THE
PERFECT
LABOR
STORM 2.0

THE PERFECT LABOR STORM 2.0

WORKFORCE TRENDS THAT WILL CHANGE THE WAY YOU DO BUSINESS

DR. IRA S. WOLFE

Updated with new chapters on Intergenerational Conflict

Published and Distributed by Ira S Wolfe and Poised for the Future Company • Lancaster, Pennsylvania USA

Editing and Copywriting: Dr. Bonnie Kerrigan Snyder, "The Writing DOC." www.thewritingdoc.com

Cover photography by iStock Images. Used by permission.

DISCLAIMER: The purpose of this book is to provide insights regarding management skills, employee motivation, and workplace improvement. It is intended only for general use and not as a specific course of treatment.

Printed in the United States of America

To order additional copies of this book, contact:
Xlibris Corporation
1-888-795-4274
www.Xlibris.com
Orders@Xlibris.com
or
Ira S. Wolfe
1-800-803-4303
www.perfectlaborstorm.com
39157

Contents

"We are about to face a demographically driven shortfall in labor that will make the late 1990's seem like a minor irritation."

Anthony Carnevale,
Former Chairman of the National Commission for Employment Policy

The Bermuda Triangle of Future Jobs

Three seemingly innocuous weather systems collided off the Atlantic coast in the spring of 1991 to produce one of the most powerful weather storms on record. This storm was subsequently described by Sebastian Junger in his book as "The Perfect Storm," which later became the movie blockbuster by the same name, starring George Clooney.

Beginning just a few years later, a similar event was being discussed in boardrooms of almost every developed group, including the United States. In the media, threats of future worker shortages became very real when the dot-com boom of the late 1990s and record low unemployment collided. Businesses could hardly find enough workers to do all the jobs that were being created. Recruitment strategies, including everything from offering large signing bonuses to tripling immigration quotas, failed to stem the pilfering of employees from other companies to fill job vacancies in their company.

Employment requirements dropped so low that jokes about "warm-body hiring" and the "mirror" test (if candidates could fog a mirror, they were hired) became standard conversation in recruiting and human resource circles.

And then it hit me. The proverbial light bulb went on—that "aha!" when the idea you've been working on finally clicks and a cascade of ideas explodes. Changes in world economics and demographic trends were beginning to collide in what was shaping up to be "The Perfect Labor Storm" (a phrase I coined in 1999).

Not unlike the *Andrea Gail,* which was sucked under by the colossal waves two days before the full force of "The Perfect Storm" even hit, many businesses and organizations were meeting a similar fate. Skilled workers were becoming harder and harder to find. While managers and business owners were hoping for a break in the clouds and praying that this storm too would pass, they failed to understand that this Perfect Labor Storm was unlike any other they ever confronted.

Even as recently as 2006, surveys suggested that most employers were not yet taking the anticipated labor shortage seriously. Their wait-and-see attitude and shortsighted strategy will surely sink their *Andrea Gails*—the businesses they captain. Human Resource professionals, executives, and managers alike wrongly believe that they are the isolated targets of some insidious plot to abscond with their workers, or

9

else that they are just magnets for underskilled employees with poor work ethics. So, they captain their ships from port to port, looking for workers.

Since the mid-1990s, I have tracked the past and future careers of workers while studying demographic and socio-economic trends. What I discovered was that behind every solution offered by economists, business leaders, and consulting gurus to solve the worker and skills shortages, there is a trapdoor. For the naive and closed-minded, only danger lies ahead.

Addressing the Lancaster County (PA) Workforce Summit in December 2006, Sandi Vito, PA Deputy Secretary for Workforce Development, warned that 1 in 5 companies will lose 40% of their top skilled workers in the coming years.

While the statistics released in the 1990s pointed to a shortage of workers, the problem has evolved and escalated. This "Perfect Labor Storm," you will see, has no industry or geographic boundaries. It is not just limited to the United States but its reach extends around the world. In his best-selling book, *The World Is Flat*, author Tom Friedman describes how traditional neighborhood services such as accounting, banking, and even food service are being out-sourced and in-sourced. From plumbers to dental hygienists to teachers to border patrol officers to radiologists, virtually every industry, at nearly every level, in every developed country, is already affected by a shortage of workers who possess the right skills and attitudes to do the jobs.

Employers in unlikely places are beginning to feel the pinch. As it turns out, the supply of worldwide qualified labor is finite. *Business Week*, in its April 9, 2007 edition, described how businesses from Peoria, Il. to Ho Chi Minh City, Vietnam to Sofia, Bulgaria are struggling to find and retain qualified workers. Eighty-two percent of companies in a Manpower, Inc. survey reported they are having trouble filling jobs for factory workers, laborers and accountants. Sixty-one percent of Japanese companies reported trouble finding sales representatives and secretaries while 36% of Canadian companies cannot find enough plumbers, electricians, welders and sales representatives. Even Chinese and Indian companies reported unfilled vacancies for lab workers, laborers, engineers, and IT staff.

Future labor shortages will not blow over. In fact, the full force of the tempest won't begin to hit until the end of this decade. According to *Business Week*, traditional workforce strategies developed for a period of surplus labor don't fit the new realities.

Consider this your "severe" weather warning, and prepare for the gathering storm.

Why This Storm Will Not Blow Over

Thanks to significant productivity gains from the late 1990s through 2006, the number of workers required to produce goods or deliver services has declined for many businesses. For instance, productivity in the U.S. during the later months of 2003 rose 9.4%. What this means is that workers in this country produced in 2000 hours what formerly took 2,188 hours. This increased productivity is equivalent to 24 fewer days needed to produce the same products and services as were required before all the layoffs, downsizing, and business closures.

This is great news for employers, who are getting more productivity with fewer people. It's not such good news for the unemployed and the employees working extra hard. A combination of doing more with less and replacing activity-driven production with technology and automation have permanently eliminated many jobs. But this doesn't mean that demand for workers won't increase. The U.S. population continues to grow. Despite slowing from the torrid 1990s, jobs continue to be created.

To run the technology, workers need to be more skilled, more innovative, and able to work at a faster pace. In the 2004 book, *The Jobs Revolution: Changing How America Works*, author Richard Riley notes that as recently as 1991, fewer than 50% of U.S. jobs required skilled workers. By 2015, it is estimated that 76% of American jobs will demand highly skilled employees. To be competitive today, businesses must employ workers who are innovative and capable of dealing with complexity at an ever-increasing pace.

"None of the top 10 jobs that will exist in 2010 exist today," says former U.S. Education Secretary Riley. Those jobs will require technology that's still being developed to solve problems that don't yet exist. The book adds: "Rather than focusing on specific technologies or specific problems, we need to equip students with those concepts that are common to all problems, all technologies, all skills, ranging from workplace engineering to ethics to entrepreneurship."

The shortage of workers has shifted from one of quantity to one of quality. Vacancies abound for positions ranging from maintenance technicians to CEOs. Recruitment efforts are intensifying, time-to-fill job vacancies is increasing, and turnover among top-performers is spinning out of control. According to statistics provided by the Bureau of Labor Statistics, the annual voluntary turnover rate in the

U.S. has increased from a low of 20.2% in 2004 to 23.4% in 2006. Skilled workers have lots of choices and many are leaving, looking for clearer skies and greener pastures.

The Metropolitan Area Employment report that the Bureau of Labor Statistics released at the end of January 2007 shows that even with lackluster GDP growth this year, employers are in for misery in a dozen major metropolitan areas when it comes to hiring help.

One example of this round two of the war for talent is an advertising firm that has been in business since 1993. It has about 100 openings that managers are scrambling to fill. That's up from 40 last summer. The headcount of the whole firm is only 300! As the owners of this business found out, you can't build a booming business unless you have the bodies to staff it.

According to an October 2006 article in the *Economist* magazine, Winston Churchill said, "The empires of the future will be empire's of the mind." That begins the new *Economist* "Survey of Talent," an international poll of senior human resources managers. Here's a snippet of what they had to say:

- 75% said that "attracting and retaining" talent was their number one priority.
- 62% worried about company-wide talent shortages.

The Corporate Executive Board also surveyed some 4,000 hiring managers in more than 30 companies, with the following findings:

- Average quality of candidates had declined by 10% since 2004
- Average time to fill a vacancy had increased from 37 days to 51 days
- Over one-third of the managers said they had hired below-average candidates "just to fill a position quickly"

As a result, salaries and wages will go up, especially for hard-to-fill positions. Bigger paychecks were cited as the number one hiring trend for 2007 in a survey conducted by CareerBuilder.com of over 2,600 hiring managers and human resources professionals in late fall 2006.

Forty percent of the surveyed employers report they currently have job openings for which they can't find qualified candidates. In response, employers are becoming more competitive in recruitment and retention efforts. Eighty percent of employers report their companies will increase salaries for existing employees. Sixty-five percent will raise compensation levels by 3% or more while nearly one in five will raise compensation levels by 5% or more. Nearly half of employers (49%) expect to increase salaries on initial offers to new employees.

To make matters worse for employers, one in three employees had recently been approached by another firm hoping to lure them away.

The "Perfect Labor Storm" has landed.

Businesses will see an increase in skilled worker shortages and more competition for the shrinking qualified pool through at least 2050. The result will be higher salaries, more training and career advancement opportunities, and more flexible work cultures.

And that's all before the brunt of boomer retirements has even begun.

The statistics are stunning. Starting in 2012, nearly 10,000 Americans will turn 65 every day. The number of workers age 55 and over is growing four times faster than the workforce as a whole. Baby boomers, who in 2006 ranged in age from 42 to 60, currently represent one-half of the U.S. workforce. This is slightly more than the combined number of workers from the succeeding two generations, Generation X and the Millennial Generation (Generation Y). In contrast, the number of workers ages 35-44 is projected to decrease by 10%.

To offset projected labor shortfalls over the next decade, the 55+ age group will need to increase its labor force participation by 20-25%.

A glimmer of hope, proposed by several economists and government leaders, is that baby boomers, the generation born between 1946 and 1964, will continue to work longer than expected. While this may be true, several critical consequences associated with more people living longer and having more active lifestyles are being ignored.

For instance, older people use more healthcare services than younger people. Insuring older workers, along with increased pension benefits, costs money. These are just two of the many reasons that millions of employees were incentivized to accept early retirement. So what has changed? If older employees now agree to work longer, who will pay for their healthcare benefits—and how will organizations afford them, especially with the downward pressures on profits caused by global competitiveness and rising wages?

Older workers will also demand more flexible work schedules for travel, personal concerns, and visiting grandchildren. Added to this is the fact that many older workers lack the high tech, communication, and problem solving skills needed to do today's jobs.

Then consider all the older workers who will have even older parents and other relatives requiring personal attention—and more and more workers will be torn out of the workplace to care for their elders. While a few may leave the workplace only temporarily, others may leave permanently.

Since 1950, the U.S. population has increased 50%. We now have 150 million more mouths to feed and people to service than we did in 1950. Between 2000 and 2030, the U.S. population will grow another 26%. By 2050, the U.S. population is projected to grow 42% to about 420 million people, according to the Population Reference Bureau.

In part, this U.S. growth will come from new births and immigration. But a significant portion will be a result of people living longer ... and longer. The segment of the population that is 65 and older will grow by more than 80%.

In the latter half of the twentieth century, the need for more workers to serve an expanding population was filled by 77 million baby boomers, who entered the workforce between 1964 and the late 1980s. Women also entered the workforce in record numbers. The participation rate for women working outside their homes increased from 34% to 60%. For women ages 25 to 64, participation exceeds 76%. This time around, we won't be able to look to women to solve the worker shortage. We've already tapped that human resource reserve, and the well is going dry.

The United States is not alone. Nearly every developed country—including England, Germany, Japan, and Italy—simply won't have enough young people to take care of their exploding aging populations.

Worker shortages won't go away even if job creation is slower than anticipated. The problem is not only that we don't have enough young replacement workers, but that the workers we have don't possess the skills required to do all the jobs available today. The writers of the article "America Isn't Ready—Here's What To Do About It" (*Fortune*: July 25, 2005) concur that the No. 1 policy prescription is education.

Over 60% of all manufacturing jobs in 1950 required unskilled labor. Today, less than 15% of all manufacturing positions are unskilled. Even as recently as 1973, blue-collar workers represented over 60% of the workforce. Shortly, just 10% of the workforce will be blue-collar. The U.S. Department of Education in 2000 projected that in the U.S. only 20% of our workers will have the skills to do 60% of the jobs.

So what's the problem? Our growing population is demanding more skilled services (healthcare and technology) faster than our ability to deliver them. According to the Employment Policy Foundation, the demand for labor over the next decade can outpace supply by as much as 35 million jobs.

But the biggest differentiator of all when compared with previous workforce shifts is that no population in history has had so many aging people live so long. What used to be a demographic pyramid, with a small number of elderly at the top and a wide base of children at the bottom, has turned into a column, or "silo", with its mid-portion, the primary workforce, showing signs of weakening (see People Pyramid on page 15).

Because of the baby bust and birth dearth of the 1970s and early 1980s, we are moving into a period of declining work-aged citizens. In the 1950s, a worker lived just a few years beyond his or her 40 or more years of company service. Today, employees are retiring and not only living 10 or 12 more years, but many are enjoying active lifestyles for 20, 30, and even 40 additional years. This is *nearly an entire extra lifetime* when compared to our 19th century ancestors!

With medical advancements, who knows how long people will really live in the future? The following graph depicts the dramatic shift in our national demographics, which is soon going to be wreaking havoc on our national workforce:

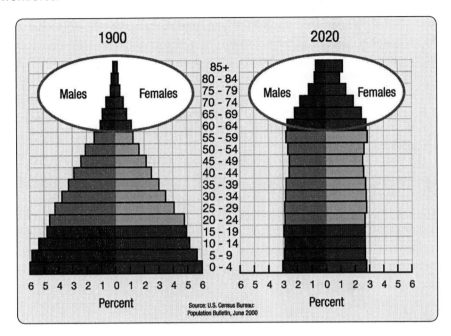

The bottom line is that jobs will continue to be plentiful for years to come, but workers will not. This brings some really bad news to those business owners and managers who think an economic recovery is the answer to their prayers. Our businesses, government, and communities have not prepared for the "aging bubble." They do not have even the faintest hint of an infrastructure or available resources that can provide all the services required to support the burgeoning "triple A" segment of population—active, affluent, and aging.

The business solution will be a continuing effort to produce more output from fewer people. But the need to increase individual productivity comes with a big price. According to a study by ComPsych, 86% of workers are experiencing job stress, and half of them described their stress as "extreme fatigue" or "feeling out of control." Other studies show that the number of employees calling in sick from stress-related factors has tripled since 1996. In the U.S., nearly 550 million working days are lost annually from stress-related absenteeism.

Stress increases already out-of-control healthcare costs. Up to 90% of all visits to primary care physicians are for stress-related complaints, and up to 80% of industrial accidents are due to stress. Combined with the fact that the average elderly American (65 years and older) consumes 37% more healthcare than the average worker, costs for healthcare will continue to skyrocket. Paradoxically, as employers attempt to shift cost-sharing to workers, health insurance will remain a top benefit, used to attract and retain the best and the brightest.

World-class businesses have already figured out that the ways of old have got to stop. Global competition and shrinking profit margins no longer allow employers to tolerate under-performing and poorly performing workers. Best practices dictate that each individual contributor, from the boardroom to the maintenance crew, must carry his or her own weight. The days of absorbing the costs of overstaffing to maintain full productivity, while continuing to pay for nonperformance, are long gone.

And that, friends, is the crux of the problem that faces U.S. employees and employers alike.

We do not and will not have enough people to fill all the jobs that will be required to provide services to, and produce goods for, a growing, aging, and demanding population. And we don't and won't have enough people with the right skills to do all the jobs that exist, even today.

On the pages that follow, I'll share the storm warnings that are gathering on the horizon—indicators of the Perfect Labor Storm—followed by solutions for recruiting and managing the four working generations.

Factor: Skilled Worker Shortages

Organizations in the United States and around the world are finding themselves ill-equipped to compete in the 21st-century economy. The reason: too many workers lack the right skills to help their employers grow and succeed. The result is a widening gap between the skills their organizations need to grow and the current capabilities of their employees.

Communities, states, regions, and entire nations pay a heavy price when businesses cannot find or equip employees with the right skills for critical jobs. Even in China and India, widely perceived as unstoppable engines of economic growth, a lack of worker skills often is cited as a major obstacle to business success.

In 2030, as 77 million baby boomers leave the workforce, there will be twice as many retirees as there are today, but only 18% more workers. The Bureau of Labor Statistics (BLS) data forecasts a shortage of *more than 10 million workers* by the year 2010. That's just around the corner. And this doesn't even take into account the skill level of these employees; those are just warm bodies. The shortage of *skilled* employees is even more dire. The looming crisis is almost too frightening to contemplate. The Hudson Institute predicts that the supply of skilled labor in the United States will not catch up to the demand until the year 2050.[1]

Eighty-three percent of more than 800 U.S. based manufacturers surveyed in the National Association of Manufacturers' *2005 Skill Gap Report* indicated a shortage of skilled manpower is already affecting their ability to serve customers. Fifty-three percent of the respondents indicated employees need to improve basic skills like attendance, timeliness and work ethics along with team-building, multi-tasking and problem solving skills.

In ASTD's 2003 white paper, The Human Capital Challenge, the ASTD Public Policy Council observed the following: "Now more than ever, the success of public and private organizations in the United States and throughout the world depends on the knowledge and capabilities of their employees."

The key to achieving business growth and success in the 21st century is having a workforce with the capacity to continually learn, update their skills, and hone their knowledge in today's rapidly changing environment.

PLS Indicators: Stats, Facts, and Trends

By 2010 we will have 167,754,000 skilled jobs to fill in the United States alone. By 2010 we will have only 157,721,000 people in the workforce to fill those jobs. Assuming that 5% of the workforce holds two jobs, we still will have approximately 2.2 million jobs unfilled.

Source: Human Trend Alerts, October 2002

The number of U.S. workers between ages 55 and 64 will grow 51% to 25 million by 2012, meaning the fastest-growing portion of the workforce is the one at most risk of retiring soon. At the same time, the number of workers between ages 35 and 44 is expected to shrink by 7%.

Source: Wall Street Journal, Sept. 20, 2005

One-fifth of this country's large, established companies will be losing 40% or more of their top-level talent in the next five years.

Source: Development Dimensions International

As 38 million baby boomers reached employment age in the 1970s and 1980s, the workplace exploded by 50%. In the decade following 2010, the portion of the population under age 45—the principal talent pool for managers and workers—will shrink by 6%.

The annual growth rate of the U.S. population ages 15-64, the traditional working age population, is projected at 0.3%. The comparable rate for ages 65 and over is projected at 3.1%. Almost 90% of the net increase in the traditional working age population is projected to occur in the age 55-64 group.

Source: The Aging of the U.S. Workforce: Employer Challenges and Responses, January 2006, Ernst & Young

Although 41 million people are expected to enter the American workforce by 2010, 46 million college-educated baby boomers will retire in the next 20 years.

More than 40% of the U.S. labor force will reach traditional retirement age by the end of the decade. At the same time, the number of workers between ages 35 and 44 is expected to shrink by 7%.

Source: Bureau of Labor Statistics

Nearly all of the 24 million people who stop working in this decade will be experienced employees who are headed into retirement.

Source: The Kiplinger Letter, May 17, 2002

The demand for labor in the next decade will outpace supply by 35 million jobs:

- In 1950, 60% of all manufacturing jobs required unskilled labor.
- By 2005, less than 15% of all manufacturing positions were unskilled.
- In 1973, blue-collar workers represented over 60% of the workforce.
- By 2000, only 10% of the workforce was blue-collar workers.

Source: Employment Policy Foundation

83% of more than 800 U.S. based manufacturers indicate a shortage of skilled manpower is affecting their ability to serve customers.

53% of the indicated employees need to improve basic skills like attendance, timeliness and work ethics along with team-building, multi-tasking and problem solving skills.

Source: National Association of Manufacturers,
2005 Skill Gap Report: A survey of the Manufacturing Workforce

By the end of the decade, 18 million jobs will require individuals with baccalaureate degrees. At current levels of graduation, we will have a shortfall of 6 million.

Source: Employment Policy Foundation

In 2003, the United States experienced its lowest recorded birthrate in history. In 1960, the baby boom peaked at an average fertility rate of 3.61 births per woman. By 2023, fertility is projected at just 1.9 children per woman.

Source: Bureau of Labor Statistics, U.S. Department of Labor

Every year, India graduates 2 million proficient English speakers with strong technical and quantitative skills. China graduated 325,000 engineers in 2004, five times as many as the U.S. The number of researchers in China reached 811,000 in 2002, compared to Japan's 676,000, European Union's 1 million, and the United States' 1.3 million.

Source: A.T. Kearney

65% of all American employment now requires specific skills.

Source: Bureau of Labor Statistics

75% of the American workforce will need to be retrained merely to retain their jobs.

Source: Bureau of Labor Statistics

Employers estimate that 39% of their current workforce and 26% of new hires will have basic skill deficiencies.

Source: Bureau of Labor Statistics

Skills that employers are increasingly demanding are the ability to work in a team, solve complex problems, and communicate clearly in print and in person.

Source: Coplin, 10 Things Employers Want You to Learn in College

Skills that will keep workers marketable in the near term are self-motivation, time management, strong oral and written communication, relationship building, salesmanship, problem solving, information evaluation, and leadership.

Source: Futurist Update, Feb 2004

In the future, even more emphasis will be placed on skills that cannot be automated—caring, judgment, intuition, ethics, inspiration, friendliness, and imagination.

Source: Futurist, Sep-Oct 2004

According to the Hudson Institute, the world's "advanced regions"—including the U.S., Western Europe, and the developed nations of the Pacific Rim—will see a smaller number of new workers entering the labor force in the current decade than were added in the 1990s. Western Europe will experience an absolute decline in workers between 2000 and 2010.

Source: "Beyond Workforce 2020: The coming (and present)
international market for labor," June 23, 2000

Where are the biggest gaps? Business leaders have reported deficiencies in both "hard" and "soft" skills among current and prospective workers. Shortages are reported in four key areas:

- Basic skills—The "three Rs" (reading, writing, and arithmetic), customer service, communications, basic business acumen
- Technical and professional skills—computer/technology skills, plus skills for specialized industries (e.g., automotive or construction)
- Management and leadership—skills covering areas such as supervision, team-building, goal-setting, planning, motivation, decision making, and ethical judgment
- Emotional intelligence—skills such as self-awareness, self-discipline, persistence, and empathy

Source: Managing the Mature Workforce/Report #1369,
The Conference Board, Sept. 19, 2005.

According to a Conference Board study, the number of U.S. workers between ages 35 and 44, those normally expected to move into senior management ranks, will decline by 10% by 2010. In Europe and Japan, the shortage of younger workers is even more pronounced.

Source: Managing the Mature Workforce/Report #1369,
The Conference Board, Sept. 19, 2005

The combination of baby boomers, immigrants, and working women has helped swell our workforce by 1.6% a year for the past 50 years. But during the coming 50 years America's workforce will grow by approximately 0.6% annually, about one-third the pace set over the last half-century.

Source: The Jobs Revolution: Changing How America Work, 2005.

Factor: No Industry Left Behind

Every industry will be competing for the same, shrinking labor pool and there is little native-born talent left from which to draw. MIT economist Laurence Kotlikoff points out that our national labor force participation rate—the proportion of all eligible people who are actually in the workforce—is near record levels at "an impressive 66.4% in spite of a soft economy. The record, established in the late 1990s, was 67.1%. In some cities and states, the figure is higher."[2] Many employees are already working far more than forty hours a week and enduring too few leisure hours and considerable stress, which is impacting their health and reducing their productivity.

You can see just how far we are stretching our current workforce by comparing the current labor force participation rate with those from earlier times. As recently as 1980, the labor force participation rate was 63.8%. It was still lower in 1970, 1960, and 1950 when the figures were 60.4%, 59.4%, and 59.2%, respectively, according to Kotlikoff.[3]

The single largest contributor to the rising participation rate is the two-earner household. Once rare, it is now the norm, making home life more hurried and stressful and limiting the time available to care for (or even to have) children. The upshot is this: the current workforce is already pushed to its limit, and the biggest demographic changes are not yet upon us.

Furthermore, the hope that America will continue to be able to import immigrant labor from other populations to cover the shortfall appears overly optimistic; due to outsourcing, skilled foreign workers are increasingly able to find high-paying jobs close to home.

PLS Indicators: Stats, Facts, and Trends

The number of U.S. Catholic sisters (nuns) has decreased from 180,000 in 1965 to 68,600 in 2005. The worst is yet to come—the majority are older than 70 and the younger generation shows little interest.

Source: Center for Applied Research in the Apostolate, Georgetown University

Half of America's scientists and engineers are 40 or older, and the average age is steadily rising.

Source: National Science Foundation

Nearly 40% of NASA employees are age 50 or older.

Source: NASA

22% of NASA workers are 55 or older. Scientists and engineers who are over 60 at the National Aeronautics and Space Administration outnumber those under 30 by nearly 3 to 1. Only 4% of NASA workers are under 30.

Source: NASA

According to the U.S.Bureau of Labor Statistics (BLS), more than 20% of the nation's 3.2 million federal employees were ages 55 or older in 2004. Within the next five years, half of the federal government's civilian workforce will be eligible for retirement.

Source: The Aging of the U.S. Workforce: Employer Challenges and Responses,
January 2006, Ernst & Young

Nearly 20% of 16.7 million state and local government employees were age 55 or older in 2004. In comparison, just over 14% of private sector workers were ages 55 or older in 2004.

Source: The Aging of the U.S. Workforce: Employer Challenges and Responses,
January 2006, Ernst & Young

Half of current federal employees will be eligible to retire between now and the end of 2008, including 70% of supervisors.

Half of the federal air traffic controllers are eligible to retire over the next nine years. 43% of the 650,000 civilians at the Department of Defense will be eligible in the next five years.

60% of federal employees are over 45, compared with 31% in the private sector.

Source: Bernard Hodes Group, Feb 2005

The U.S. Department of Defense needs to hire more than 14,000 scientists and engineers in each of the next two years. The problem is that the pool of candidates is shrinking.

- More than half of science and engineering graduates from American universities are foreign nationals, off-limits to federal agencies.
- Fewer American students are entering science and tech fields.
- DOD must compete with the private sector and other government agencies.

The Census Bureau estimates that the overall pool who would be in the military's prime target age has shrunk as Americans age. There were 1 million fewer 18- to 24-year-olds in 2004 than in 2000.

Out of 32 million Americans age 17 to 24, many do not qualify to serve in the military. 2.3 million qualify for medical or misdemeanor waivers, 2.6 million disqualify due to medical problems, and 4.6 million are disqualified for criminal history, obesity, and dependents.

Source: U.S. Army

Trucking executives are having a tough time filling jobs in the United States, according to the *San Francisco Examiner*. Competing industries such as construction are paying more, and driving 500 miles a day can be lonely and sometimes stressful. J.B. Hunt CEO Kirk Thompson says, "Growth is at a virtual standstill until additional truck drivers are attracted."

According to the *Tulsa World*, trucking companies are trying to combat the 105 to 110% turnover rates with higher wages and signing bonuses. But drivers are less concerned about money than about being treated with honesty and respect.

Truck driver shortages are expected to worsen in coming years since about 219,000 of the country's 1.3 million long-haul truckers are over 55 and are likely to retire in the next ten years.

Source: American Trucking Association

The number of truck drivers who are not white males increased to 30% in 2004, up from 26.6% in 2001. Hispanics now account for 15% of all truck drivers, up from 12% during the same period.

Source: Department of Labor

Two-thirds of the nation's mathematics and science teaching force will retire by 2010.

Source: National Commission on Mathematics and Science Teaching for the 21st Century

40% of the current public school teaching force expects not to be teaching five years from now.

Source: Profile of Teachers in the U.S. 2005

The K-12 teaching force is aging rapidly. The proportion of K-12 teachers who are 50 years of age and older has risen from one in four (24%) in 1996 to 42% in 2005.

Source: Profile of Teachers in the U.S. 2005

Teacher attrition is expected to average about 8% per year in the next five years.

Source: Profile of Teachers in the U.S. 2005

One in five (22%) public school teachers expects to be retired five years from now. 12% expect to be in an education job other than K-12 teaching.

Source: Profile of Teachers in the U.S. 2005

Half (50%) of current high school teachers expect not to be teaching in K-12 schools in 2010. One-third (34%) of high school teachers plan to be retired by then.

Source: Profile of Teachers in the U.S. 2005

By 2010, nearly 30%, or 765,000, of our nation's public school teachers will retire.

Source: U.S. Dept. of Education

Nearly half of all college presidents (49.3%) are now older than age 60. In 1986, the number was only 13.9%.

Source: USA Today

Nearly 75% of U.S. hospital emergency departments report a shortage of specialists such as neurosurgeons and orthopedists.

Source: American College of Emergency Physicians, 2006

The demand for intensive care physicians will continue to exceed available supply through the year 2020 if current supply and demand trends continue.

Source: Department of Health and Human Services
Administration Report, 2006

The U.S. had a shortage of 1,200 critical care doctors in 2000. The HRSA report projected the shortage will rise to 1,500 in 2020.

Source: Department of Health and Human Services
Administration Report, 2006

India employs about 1.3 million IT workers. The demand for skilled workers in India is expected to rise 10% to 12% per year in the next five years.

Source: Nasscom

Factor: Aging

The coming labor storm is an inevitable part of the greatest demographic change in human history. The crisis we face is unprecedented, and will shake American—and world—institutions to their foundations. Social Security planners are quaking in their boots, trying to figure out how they are going to fund the promised retirement payouts to the largest generation in American history on the backs of fewer and fewer children—the Baby Bust generation. As Baby Boomers reach retirement age, the 20-35 year old age group directly behind them is significantly smaller, about 16% fewer in number, according to reports published in the *Atlanta Business Chronicle*.

That's just part of the problem, however. Thanks to improvements in health care and gains in longevity, future retirees can be expected to live longer than ever, increasing the economic burden of funding their lengthy retirements (and paying for their healthcare through Medicare.) Many seniors may now live in retirement thirty or even forty years.

It's not just the United States that is in demographic trouble, however. All of Europe and Japan are in the same metaphorical boat, and their situation is even more dire. At least in the U.S., our birthrates have stabilized at near the replacement level. Most of Europe has birthrates well below that, with even higher levels of promised governmental payouts. Consider this startling fact: if current low birthrate and longevity trends continue on the same path, by 2050 the number of older persons in the world would exceed the number of children *for the first time in history*.[4]

This means that our workforce is aging as well. Indeed, as reported in the *Atlanta Business Chronicle*, the median age of the labor force in 2010 will rise to its highest level since 1962—almost 41 years. As economist Laurence Kotlikoff warns, get ready to live in a world where walkers outnumber strollers. The alarm bells are sounding, but unfortunately too many leaders in business and the government have their heads in the sand; they simply are not ready to face up to the tremendous challenges that lie ahead.

PLS Indicators: Stats, Facts, and Trends

The statistics are stunning. Starting in 2012, nearly 10,000 Americans will turn 65 every day. 20% of the population, 71 million people, will be 65 or older in 2030. The total number of Americans over age 65 and eligible for Medicare will double to over 70 million within this generation, while the population over age 85 will increase nearly five-fold, to almost 19 million, by mid-century.

Source: Social Security Administration

Our society is aging as well. Between 1870 and 1990, the number of U.S. citizens aged 65 and older grew from 1 million to approximately 32 million. By 2030, the proportion of people over 65 will be 20% of the population.

Source: U.S. Census

The following chart creates a striking visual, highlighting the changing demographics. Pay particular attention to the decades between 2000 and 2030, comparing the shrinking age 20-64 groups and the explosive growth in the 65 and older populations.

Projected percentage of the population represented by each age group, 2000-2050

Age	2000	2010	2020	2030	2040	2050
0-4	6.8	6.9	6.8	6.7	6.7	6.7
5-19	21.7	20.0	19.6	19.5	19.2	19.3
20-44	36.9	33.8	32.3	31.6	31.0	31.2
45-64	22.1	26.2	24.9	22.6	22.6	22.2
65-84	10.9	11.0	14.1	17.0	16.5	15.7
85+	1.5	2.0	2.2	2.6	3.9	5.0
Source: U.S. Census Bureau						

The labor force of 16- to 19-year-olds was 7.8 million in 1990, 8.3 million in 2000, and 7.2 million in 2005; it is projected to decrease until 2020 and then gradually increase, reaching 7.2 million again in 2050.

Source: Monthly Labor Review

As a result of an aging society and more active lifestyles for "older" Americans, the above 55-years-old crowd is described as follows: aging boomer (ages 55-64), young-old (ages 65-74), old-old (ages 75-84), and oldest old (ages 85 up).
By 2012, nearly 20% of the total U.S. workforce will be 55 or older, up from just under 13% in 2000.

Source: "Labor Force Projections to 2012:
The Graying of the U.S. Workforce," Monthly Labor Review, February 2004

By 2030, 1 in 5 persons in the United States will be elderly. The number of workers age 55 and over is growing four times faster than the workforce as a whole. Baby boomers, who in 2006 ranged in age from 42 to 60, currently represent one-half of the

U.S. workforce. This is slightly more than the combined number of workers from the succeeding two generations, Generation X and Millennial Generation (Generation Y).

Source: The Aging of the U.S. Workforce: Employer Challenges and Responses, January 2006, Ernst & Young

The share of the *youth (16 to 24 years)* workforce is projected to decrease until 2020 and to grow very slowly after that.

Source: Monthly Labor Review

The share of the *prime-age (25 to 54 years)* workforce is projected to decline up to 2020 and to grow slowly after that date.

Source: Monthly Labor Review

China's Generation Y accounts for nearly one-sixth of the Chinese population, equivalent to two-thirds of the entire U.S. population. Generation Y as a percentage of the working population will increase from 17% to 28% in India, from 17% to 25% in Brazil, from 12% to 23% in China, from 14% to 28% in Russia and from 12% to 23% in the United States.

By 2025 more than 75% of the workforce in India will be from Generation Y and younger generations, while in Brazil the same cohorts will constitute more than 60% of the workforce. In the United States, Gen Y and younger will make up just less than 60%.

Source: Deloitte Research, based on United Nationals Department of Economic and Social Affairs, Population Division, Population Estimates and Projections (New York: 2005

The aging of the workforce is even more pronounced in Western Europe. By 2040 the median age of the population will be 52 years compared to the 36 years in the United States. One out of every four agricultural jobs is held by an illegal immigrant; 17% of all office and housecleaning positions, 14% of construction jobs, and 12% of food preparation jobs also are held by undocumented workers.

Source: Pew Hispanic Center, 2006

Between 2000 and 2010, the number of U.S. workers ages 45-54 is projected to grow by just over 20%, while the number of those ages 55-64 is projected to grow more than 50%. In contrast, the number of workers ages 35-44 is projected to decrease by 10%.

Source: The Aging of the U.S. Workforce: Employer Challenges and Responses, January 2006, Ernst & Young

The percentage of people 55-64 will increase by more than 50% between 2000 and 2010, while the number of people 35-44 will decline by more than 10%.

Source: Atlanta Business Chronicle

Today out of a total population of nearly 300 million, approximately 35.9 million people are age 65 or older, or about 1 of every 8 Americans. By the year 2030, people age 65 and older are projected to make up 24% of the population, nearly 1 of every 4 Americans.

Source: The Aging of the U.S. Workforce: Employer Challenges and Responses, January 2006, Ernst & Young

The labor force participation rate of 16- to 19-year-olds was 53.7% in 1990, declined to 52.0% in 2000, and fell further to 43.7% in 2005. The Bureau projects that the downward trend in the participation rate of 16- to 19-year-olds will continue and the rate will reach 34.5% in 2050. This is mainly due to increased rates of school attendance.

Source: Monthly Labor Review

According to the U.S. Bureau of Labor Statistics, more than 25% of the working population will reach retirement age by 2010, resulting in a potential worker shortage of nearly 10 million.

According to the U.S. Census Bureau, the number of people aged 55 and older will increase by 73% by 2020, while the number of younger workers will grow only 5%.

There are now more people over 90 or 100 than in all of American history put together.

In 1950, there were 7 working age people for every elderly person in the United States. By 2030, there will be only 3.

Since 1950, the number of people aged 65 and older in the United States has increased from 8% to 12%.

By 2008, the number of young adult workers, from 25- to 40-year-olds, will DECLINE by 1.7 million. That's 1.7 million fewer workers to replace the nearly 77 million baby boomers who will be eligible for retirement.

The 50 and older population from 2000-2050 will grow at a rate 68 times faster than the rate of growth for the total population.

Source: Beyond Workforce 2020, Hudson Institute

Nationally, 14% of the workforce is 55 or older.

Source: BLS

Of all the age groups, prime-aged workers aged 25 to 54 years have the strongest ties to the labor market. The group's participation rate was 83.5% in 1990, 84.0% in 2000, and 82.8% in 2005. The rate is projected to be 83.4% in 2050.

Source: Monthly Labor Review

By the middle of this century, there will be more older people than children on the planet for the first time in human history.

Source: AARP Global Aging Program

The labor force participation rate of 20- to 24-year-olds was 77.8% in both 1990 and 2000. In 2005, the rate declined significantly, to 74.6%. The participation rate of the 20- to 24-year age group is projected to decrease further, to 73.8% in 2020, and 73.1% in 2050. The decrease in the labor force participation rate of youths—especially 16- to 19-year-old men—has been a major contributor to the decrease in the overall labor force participation rate.

Source: Monthly Labor Review

As of 2004, there were 73.4 million people younger than 18 in the U.S., or approximately 25% of the population. In 1970, the percentage of kids under 18 was 34%. By 2010, the number will be only 24%.

Source: childstats.gov

In 1990, there were 37,306 Americans who were at least 100 years old. By the year 2010, there will be 131,000. And, by 2050, projections by the U.S. Census Bureau anticipate there being 834,000 centenarians. To put that figure in perspective, those 834,000 people who will be at least 100 years old in 2050 would outnumber the current populations of cities such as Baltimore, Indianapolis, San Francisco, Boston, or Denver. In fact, they would surpass the populations of all but the top 11 U.S. cities counted in the 2000 Census.

The share of the labor force aged 55 and older is rising rapidly. By 2020, the share of the labor force held by those 55 years and older is projected to be nearly 24%.

Source: Monthly Labor Review

The workplace makeup has changed dramatically from just a decade ago. In 1996 there were 64 million U.S. workers between the ages of 30 and 39 and only 43 million ages 40 to 59. Now the situation has reversed. As of June 2006 there were only 40 million ages 30 to 39 and 69 million workers 40 to 59.

Source: Bureau of Labor Statistics

Factor: Aging Stresses Ailing Healthcare System

The United States spends more on health care than any other nation on earth. As our population ages, so will our cost of providing healthcare services to infirm seniors. Shortages of healthcare workers, already at dangerously high levels, will only get worse in the coming years. In fact, the current labor shortages facing the healthcare system are indicative of the kinds of shortages that will soon be facing other industries, so pay attention to them.

Right now the biggest shortages are among registered nurses, with over 126,000 unfilled openings, nationwide. These figures are expected to worsen. According to Fitch Inc., a Wall Street Bond Rating Firm, there will be a shortfall of approximately 1 million nurses by 2010 and 1.5 million by 2020.[5] Other estimates put the number at half that, which is hardly comforting. Regardless of the exact numbers in the projections, we have to ask: who will take care of the largest generation of ailing elderly in the history of our country? It is also frightening to consider the impact of overwork on declining numbers of medical personnel; mistakes are bound to increase and the quality of patient care will decline.

It's not just nurses who are in short supply, however. There are *already* shortages exceeding 10% for imaging technicians (15.3%), licensed practical nurses (12.9%), and pharmacists (12.7%), and these shortages will only increase in the years ahead. Couple the anticipated labor shortages with the oncoming demand for services and the age-old laws of supply and demand tell us to prepare for the inevitable: rising costs and declining quality.

PLS Indicators: Stats, Facts, and Trends

Retaining older workers longer is often recommended as the solution to postponing the brain drain—the loss of knowledge and experienced workers resulting from retirement. But retaining older workers bring a new set of challenges to employers: aches, pains, and high healthcare costs.

13% of the U.S. population is 65 years and older, yet they account for 36% of the total national healthcare expenditures, 36% of hospital admissions, and 50% of all days in the hospital.

Source: Committee for Economic Development

Active adults (adults over 60) account for 60% of all healthcare spending.
Active adults purchase 70% of all prescriptions.
Active adults purchase 51% of all over-the-counter drugs.

Source: Agelight

The total expenditures for healthcare from the age of 65 until death at 90 years increases from $31,181 to $200,000.

Source: Committee for Economic Development

The aging of the healthcare workforce raises concerns that many health professionals will retire about the same time that demand for their services is increasing. Furthermore, the declining proportion of the population age 18 to 30 raises concerns regarding the ability to attract a sufficient number of new health workers.

Source: HRSA

In 2000, physicians spent an estimated 32% of patient care hours providing services to the age 65 and older population. If current consumption patterns continue, this percentage could increase to 39% by 2020.

Source: HRSA

The aging population will increase the demand for physicians per thousand population from 2.8 in 2000 to 3.1 in 2020. Demand for full-time-equivalent (FTE) registered nurses per thousand population would increase from 7 to 7.5 during this same period.

Source: HRSA

The aging population could result in rising average patient acuity, which could in turn require higher nurse and physician staffing levels.

Source: HRSA

Employees age 50 to 65 use on average from 1.4 to 2.2 times as much healthcare as workers in their 30s and 40s.

The Business Case for Workers Age 50+, 2005

The amount of time workers age 40 and older miss due to an injury or illness is greater by nearly a third than time off by younger workers.

Source: UnumProvident, Health & Productivity in the
Aging American Work Force; Realities and Opportunities

Workers older than age 40 account for 50% of all short-term disability claims and up to 75% of long-term disability claims. Primary reasons for long-term work disruptions for age 40 and older include impairments of the musculoskeletal and circulatory systems, as well as mental and cancer disorders.

Source: UnumProvident, Health & Productivity in the
Aging American Work Force; Realities and Opportunities

Additional risk factors such as smoking, lack of exercise and obesity can result in healthcare costs for workers age 40 and older that are nearly 300% higher than the younger workforce.

Source: UnumProvident, Health & Productivity in the
Aging American Work Force; Realities and Opportunities

Lost productivity of caregivers accounts for $36 billion.

American businesses spend $61 billion a year on Alzheimer's Disease. This amount is equivalent to the net profits of the top 10 Fortune 500 companies.

The number of people with Alzheimer's in the workplace will explode from 4 million today to 14 million in the next 50 years.

Source: Alzheimer's Disease: The Costs to U.S. Businesses in 2002

The average credit card debt for Americans between the ages of 65 and 69 rose 217% between 1992 and 2001, and experts suggest that this trend is part of the reason for an increase in bankruptcy filings among the elderly. A report in 2006 suggests that older Americans are using credit cards as a "plastic safety net" in the face of incomes not keeping pace with the cost of living, higher housing costs, out of pocket medical expenses, and rising property taxes.

Source: National Consumer Law Center (NCLC), 2006

Americans over the age of 55 are filing for bankruptcy at a faster rate than the general population as growing mortgage debt and higher health care costs make them more vulnerable, an American Bankruptcy Institute (2007) study shows.

The trend of rising bankruptcies among older Americans is likely to continue for the foreseeable future. The study found that rising costs for housing and health care, especially prescription drugs, have made older Americans more dependent on credit. This, in turn, makes them more vulnerable to financial rough spots.

Source: American Bankruptcy Institute Journal, May 2007

Factor: Employee Turnover

The changing demographic landscape carries another risk for employers: increasing turnover rates. Younger workers have always had higher turnover rates than older workers, and they are more likely to "jump ship" when an attractive offer comes their way. There are going to be a lot of attractive offers for these younger workers in the future job market, and the percentage of older, more stable employees will decline considerably with the retirement of the Baby Boomers.

The costs of high employee turnover can be devastating to your organization. Many of these costs are tangible: temporary replacements, severance and benefits continuation, increased unemployment insurance rates, classified advertisements, internal recruiters, hiring departments, administrative cost of handling resumes, internal candidate interviews, drug screens, and background checks.

As bad as this seems, the intangible costs can be even higher: lost productivity, wasted time, cost of training, lost departmental productivity, lost knowledge and skills, lost customer relationships, and time spent locating and developing a new hire.

PLS Indicators: Stats, Facts, and Trends

The cost to hire replacement workers is enormous and varies based on industry and geography. A sampling of available studies demonstrate the high cost as well as variability:

- $ 1,128.00 Average cost to hire a new employee (Wyatt Data Services)
- $ 2,427.00 Average cost to hire a new employee (Saratoga Institute)
- $ 10,000.00 Cost to hire a new employee stated by 45% of the surveyed employers (William H. Mercer)
- $ 2,328.00 Cost to hire a new non-exempt employee (Employment Management Association of the Society for Human Resource Management)
- $ 9,328.00 Cost to hire a new exempt employee (Employment Management Association of the Society for Human Resource Management)

Despite the drain on the bottom line, less than one-third of businesses actually track the cost-to-hire an employee. A study conducted by my firm, Success Performance Solutions, in early 2007 revealed that less than 12% of small businesses tracked their recruitment costs.

All of these costs are bound to increase as employers face the coming double blow of a seller's job market coupled with a younger, more unstable workforce. In the coming Labor Storm, finding qualified employees is only going to be half the battle. Keeping them will be equally difficult, as competitors and headhunters vie for their talents in the shrinking labor pool.

Annual voluntary turnover rates in the U.S.:

2002	2003	2004	2005	2006
20.9%	20.29%	20.20%	22.7%	23.4%

Source: Bureau of Labor Statistics, Office of Occupational Statistics and Employment Projections

Lower levels of commitment to employers by younger workers has caused the average job tenure in the United States to drop from 4.6 years in 1990 to 3.5 years in 2000.

Source: Impending Crisis

Employee Turnover Rates by Industry 2006

Total:	23.4%
Private Industry	26.5%
Natural Resources and Mining	17.0%
Construction	28.7%
Manufacturing	16.5%
Retail	34.7%
Finance	16.4%
Real Estate	19.6%
Professional and Business Services	27.8%
Education	18.6%
Heath care and Social Assistance	19.6%
Leisure and Hospitality	52.2%
Arts, Entertainment, and Recreation	28.7%
Accommodation and Food Services	56.4%

Source: Bureau of Labor Statistics, Office of Occupational Statistics and Employment Projections

The average cost to a company for a manager or professional who leaves is 18 months of salary.

Source: The Power of Nice

Median tenure for employees ages 55 to 64 was 9.3 years in January 2006, about three times the tenure for workers ages 25 to 34 (2.9 years.)

Source: Bureau of Labor Statistics

About 24% of employees age 16 and over had 12 months or less of tenure with their current employer in January 2006.

Source: Bureau of Labor Statistics

Wage and salary workers in the public sector have almost double the median tenure of private sector employees, 6.9 versus 3.6 years. One factor behind this difference is age. About 75% of government workers were age 35 and over compared with about 60% of private wage and salary workers.

Source: Bureau of Labor Statistics

The cost to replace skilled people can range from 30% to 200% of their annual salary.

Source: Impending Crisis

Within the private sector, workers in manufacturing had the highest tenure among major industries, at 5.5 years in January 2006. By comparison, workers in leisure and hospitality had the lowest median tenure (1.9 years).

Source: Bureau of Labor Statistics

Among the major occupations, workers in management, professional, and related occupations had the highest median tenure (5.2 years) in January 2006.

Source: Bureau of Labor Statistics

Within this group, employees with jobs in architectural and engineering occupations (6.5 years) and management occupations (6.0 years) had the longest tenure.

Source: Department of Labor

Workers in service occupations, who are generally younger than persons employed in management, professional, and related occupations, had the lowest median tenure (2.8 years).

Source: Department of Labor

Among employees working in service occupations, food service workers had the lowest median tenure at 1.8 years.

Source: Department of Labor

The median number of years that wage and salary workers had been with their current employer was 4.0 years in January 2006, according to the Bureau of Labor Statistics of the U.S. Department of Labor.

In January 2006, median tenure for men was 4.1 years, little different than that of women (3.9 years). From 1996 to 2002, the median tenure for men was about 0.5 year higher than for women.

The average employee in his or her late twenties has already switched jobs five or six times.

Source: Fortune

77% of Gen Xers say they'd quit in a minute if offered "increased intellectual stimulation" at a different company; 51% would jump ship for the chance to telecommute; and 61% of Gen X women would leave their current jobs if they were offered more flexible hours elsewhere.

Source: The NeXt Revolution, as cited in Fortune

35%-40% of today's workers are actively looking for another job.

Source: The Herman Group

Federal labor statistics show that workers in almost every age group are staying at jobs for a shorter period of time than their counterparts did in the 1980s. For instance, 25- to 34-year-olds have held their current jobs for a median of 2.7 years, down from 3 years in 1983.

Source: San Francisco Chronicle

Factor: Obesity

The American worker is under a great deal of stress. Asked to increase productivity continually, and to make do with less, workers put in more and more hours on the job. In the short run, this may seem to be an efficient course; in the long run, however, increased workloads come with their own associated costs. One of these is obesity. Pressured employees work through lunch hour, eating high fat, fast food "meals" (perhaps purchased from a nearby vending machine) at their desks, in order to "get more done." It is the rare worker indeed who goes home at five o'clock to a healthy, home-cooked meal prepared by a stay-at-home spouse. Time to exercise, or even to throw a ball in the yard with children, is in increasingly short supply.

Juliet Schor, a professor of Economics at Harvard University, wrote poignantly about increased pressure on American workers in her book, *The Overworked American*. Schor points out that in the last twenty years, the number of hours an American worker spends at work has steadily increased to the point of adding an additional day each year. American workers currently work 320 hours, or two more months, than workers in France or Germany. The amount of time spent at work has increased for all industries, for men and women, married and single. Along with the increase in time spent at work is the constant feeling of being rushed and neglect for our personal health. The physical result is evident all around us: increased obesity rates among American workers.

These rising obesity rates show up in the bottom line through declining productivity and mounting healthcare bills. Obesity also contributes to depression, diabetes, and a host of other ailments that debilitates the workforce. Alarming obesity rates among American children (nearly unheard of decades ago when children went outside to play under the supervision of their stay-at-home parent) also bode ill for future productivity rates of American workers.

PLS Indicators: Stats, Facts, and Trends

Four studies linking obesity to increased employer costs for health care and workers compensation were released recently.

One, conducted by the Medstat Group Inc. showed that moderate and severe obesity were linked to annual health care cost increases of 21% and

75%, respectively. Moderate obesity was associated with a $670 increase in costs, and severe obesity resulted in a $2,441 increase in costs.

Another study examining records of nearly 12,000 workers by Duke University Medical Center linked obesity to higher medical costs and 13 times the number of lost work days than non-obese workers. Also, the study found that obese workers averaged 11.65 workers compensation claims per 100 workers, while non-obese employees filed an average of 5.8 claims per 100 workers. As a result, obese employees had medical costs seven times higher, for an average of $51,019 per 100 employees. The most common causes of injury among obese workers were slips, falls and attempts to lift something.

In a third study, CCH reports that researchers at the Johns Hopkins Bloomberg School of Public Health Center for Injury Research and Policy recently published a study in the American Journal of Epidemiology showing that obesity increases the risk of traumatic workplace injury. Of the 7,690 workers included in the study, 29% were injured at least once between January 2, 2002, and December 31, 2004. Approximately 85% of the injured workers were classified as overweight or obese.

Finally, using data provided by nine large companies, Thomson Healthcare, found a severly obese employee typically runs up a tab of $5,695 a year in medical care and pharmacy costs, 75% more than a worker of normal weight.

Nearly 30% of the U.S. adult population is obese; in 1991, only 12% of the population was obese.
Source: HR Magazine, March 2004 and An Economic Analysis of Adult Obesity

Obesity costs U.S. companies an estimated $12.7 billion annually.
Source: National Business Group on Health

Obesity is estimated to account for 43% of all healthcare spending by U.S. businesses on coronary heart disease, hypertension, type 2 diabetes, hypercholesterolemia, stroke, gall bladder disease, osteoarthritis of the knee, and endometrial cancer.
Source: The Business Case for Weight/Obesity Management,
www.leadehealth.com

The most obese workers (those 100 or more pounds too heavy) make up 3% of the employed population but account for 21% of the costs of obesity. The number of people with extreme obesity has doubled over the past 10 years.
Source: RTI International and Centers for Disease Control and Prevention

An estimated 65% of U.S. adults over the age of 20 are obese or overweight. Obesity now affects 29% of workers. The cost to employers is significant—approximately 9% of U.S. healthcare costs, about $123 billion—are due to obesity and excess weight. The productivity loss associated with obesity is even higher than what has been reported for tobacco use.

Source: The Business Case for Weight/Obesity Management,
www.leadehealth.com

Since the late 1970s, the number of obese adults in the United States has grown over 50%.
Source: An Economic Analysis of Adult Obesity

Overweight workers cost their bosses more in injury claims than their lean counterparts. The heaviest employees had twice the rate of workers' compensation claims as their fit co-workers. The most obese workers—those with BMIs of 40 or higher—had the highest rates of claims and lost workdays.
Source: National Institute for Occupational Safety and Health

In 1991, in the U.S., only four states had an obesity prevalence of 15 to 19%. No state had an obesity prevalence of 20% or more. In 2003, 15 states had an obesity prevalence of 15% to 19% and four states had a prevalence of 25% or more.
Source: U.S. Centers for Disease Control

The annual costs of medical treatment for obesity have been estimated at nearly $100 billion or $732 higher on average for obese people than for people of normal weight.
Source: An Economic Analysis of Adult Obesity

Approximately half of the estimated $78.5 billion in medical care spending in 1998 attributable to excess body weight was financed through private insurance (38%) and patient out-of-pocket payments (14%).
Source: An Economic Analysis of Adult Obesity

From 1997 to 2002, Americans' private spending on obesity-linked medical problems increased from $3.6 billion to $36.5 billion and swelled from 2% of all health spending to 11.6%. The rise in obesity has boosted the costs for treating arthritis, asthma, diabetes, and heart disease, costing $1,244 more than treating a healthy-weight person.

Higher expenses for obesity are absorbed:

- By employees, who end up paying higher healthcare premiums.

- By employers, who pick up a larger share of insurance costs, pay higher premiums, or hire replacement workers.
- By obese employees themselves, if they aren't paid for their time off or don't have insurance coverage.

Source: Health Affairs

Obese employees are twice as likely to be absent 14 or more times per year.

Source: HR Magazine, March 2004

Obesity is associated with 39 million lost workdays.

Source: HR Magazine, March 2004

Paid sick leave associated with obesity costs employers an estimated $2.4 billion per year.

Source: HR Magazine, March 2004

Obese workers have the highest prevalence of work limitations, with 6.9% experiencing work limitations versus 3.0% among normal-weight workers. 25% of obese workers under-perform because of infirmities related to their weight.

Source: HR Magazine, March 2004

Obesity is associated with 239 million restricted activity days.

Source: HR Magazine, March 2004 and The Business Case for Weight/Obesity Management, www.leadehealth.com

Obesity-related disability claims cost an average of $8,720 per employee per year.

Source: UnumProvident

The percentage of Americans ages 65 to 74 who are obese has risen from 18% to 36% over the past 2 decades, according to a federal study ... and 40% of boomers are obese.

Source: The Business Case for Weight/Obesity Management, www.leadehealth.com

If obesity trends continue through 2020, without other changes in health behaviors or medical technology, the proportion of people age 50-69 with disabilities (those who are limited in their ability to care for themselves or perform other routine tasks) will increase by 18% for men and by 22% for women.

Source: The Business Case for Weight/Obesity Management, www.leadehealth.com

Obesity's co-epidemic, type 2 diabetes, has increased six-fold in the last 5 decades. An estimated 14% of persons over the age of 20 have diagnosed diabetes, undiagnosed diabetes, or impaired fasting glucose.

Source: The Business Case for Weight/Obesity Management,
www.leadehealth.com

Factor: Education and Literacy

When we speak of the coming labor shortages, we are discussing raw numbers—warm bodies. If you consider the number of *educated* and *skilled* workers that will be available to future recruiters, the actual shortfall will be worse. Many employers are finding that potential new employees are sorely lacking in required educational competencies. Basic literacy and numeracy skills are a growing problem among recent graduates of both high schools *and* colleges.

Couple that with rising dropout rates—currently, about 1.3 million students drop out of high school each year—to appreciate the magnitude of the problem. The number of dropouts has grown over the past thirty years; according to the National Center for Education Statistics, the population segment of U.S. 16- through 24-year-olds who were not enrolled in school or who did not have a high school diploma or a GED credential was about 11% in 2001. This number can be expected to grow as increasing numbers of young people recognize that there are ample jobs available to them without completing their diploma or degree.

The following statistics demonstrate the urgency with which employers are going to have to fight to recruit and retain "the best and the brightest" of the future American workforce:

PLS Indicators: Stats, Facts, and Trends

We are in a race for IQ points. The countries (and companies) that accumulate the most IQ points win. In the race for IQ points, the kinds of jobs we produce will be different.

- Jobs are declining in the following industries: Timber (-32%); Farm Workers (-20%); Sewing (-50%); Typesetters (-62%).
- Jobs will be created in the following positions: Electrical Engineers (+28%); Medical Sciences (+33%); Architects (+44%); Legal Assistants (+66%); Financial Services (+78%).

Source: Todd Buchholz, Bringing the Jobs Home

Thirty years ago, the U.S. had 30% of the world's college population. Today that number is 14%.

Source: National Center on Education and the Economy,
"Tough Choices or Tough Times," 2007

For every 100 ninth graders:

- 68 graduate from high school in four years.
- 40 enroll directly in college after graduation
- 27 are still enrolled in college one year after entering
- 18 earn an associate degree within three years or a bachelor's degree within six years
- 82 don't receive a college degree

Source: National Center on Education and the Economy,
"Tough choices or Tough Times," 2007

The looming shortage of skilled workers is keeping most execs awake at night.

Source: A study released in 2006 by the International Association
for Human Resource Information

The International Association for Human Resource Information reports that 77% of their HR respondents cite talent management initiatives as a top priority for the next three years. A lot of focus is on training current staff for new roles, rather than hiring for new skills.

More than 75% of the workforce must be retrained to keep the jobs they have; 80% of jobs will require some sort of postsecondary education; 61% will require more than a high school education but less than a bachelor's degree.

Source: U.S. Department of Labor

A decade ago, the United States had the highest overall graduation rates at the bachelor's level. Today there are fewer U.S. entrants in these programs than the Organization for Economic Co-operation and Development averages.

Source: Organization for Economic Co-operation and Development

According to the U.S. Census Bureau, one of the largest and fastest-growing groups of young people in the United States is dropouts, rising to almost 1 out of 3 Americans in their mid-20s.

Source: Organization for Economic Co-operation and Development

Though there are more than 9 million males ages 17 to 21 in the U.S., only about 1 in 3 have the educational and other qualifications needed to become a member of the armed forces. And of those 3 million qualified males, about half already are in the military or in college.

U.S. business and industry leaders estimate spending an average of $600 million per year on remedial reading, writing, and math skills training for employees.

Source: National Institute for Literacy,
Literacy Skills for 21st Century America

U.S. high school students are getting their lunches eaten when it comes to math and science scores compared to the most advanced economies of Europe and Asia. On the recently released National Assessment of Educational Progress exams, 39% of white eighth graders were proficient in reading vs. just 15% of Hispanics and 12% of blacks.

In 2002, just 68% of high school students graduated 4 years after they started ninth grade. That's down from 75% in the early 1980s. And just 10% of students from the bottom quartile of family income brackets earn a BA by the time they're 24 vs. 81% from the top quartile.

Source: Nation at Risk

Students in the United States finished in the bottom of mathematics skills when compared to students in 40 surveyed countries. Yet 72% of the US students said they got good grades in math, more than any other country.

The United States ranked 28th of 40 countries in math and 18th in reading when comparing outcomes per dollar spent on education.

Source: Organization for Economic Cooperation and Development

The U.S. Department of Education reports that over the next decade, more than two million new teachers will walk into a classroom for their first day. Unfortunately, as the National Center for Education Statistics found, 666,000 of those new teachers will leave sometime during the first 3 years of teaching and one million of them will not make it past 5 years.

The cost of high teacher turnover and attrition rates is enormous. Every year, American schools spend $2.6 billion on teacher attrition.

Between the end of the 1999-2000 school year and the beginning of the 2000-2001 school year, approximately 67,000 teachers retired, accounting for only 12% of the total turnover of 546,000 during that period. The data show that the demand for new teachers, and subsequent staffing difficulties, are primarily due to pre-retirement teacher turnover.

Source: U.S. Department of Education

According to a National Center for Education Statistics (NCES) survey of 8,400 public and private school teachers, the main reasons for high teacher turnover and attrition rates are inadequate administrative support (38%) and workplace conditions (32%). Two-thirds of employers said that public school students don't have the basic cognitive skills to succeed. One-third of the employers said the recent graduates had poor writing skills and 23% had poor math skills. One-third also said that young workers have problems with punctuality and poor attitude.

Source: Yankelovich Partners, 2005

In 2002, almost 35% of high school graduates in the U.S. did not go on to attend a four-year institution or a two-year college program. That's 972,000 high school grads. Of those 972,000, 131,000 were unemployed and 197,000 (35% of the 35% not working) were not even in the labor force. By 2020 we're going to have a shortfall of some 14 million skilled workers who will need some type of post-secondary education or training to qualify for the high skilled jobs our economy demands. In fact, 80% of the U.S.'s fastest-growing jobs over the next decade will require at least two years of college. Think of that—80%!

The number of women obtaining degrees is outpacing that of men. Women obtained between 40% and 60% of the bachelor's degrees in mathematics and sciences in 2000.

Only 36% of doctorate-level faculty in the U.S. are currently under 45 years of age.

If you come from a family earning over $96,000 a year, your odds of getting a bachelor's degree by age 24 are 1 in 2. If you come from a family earning under $36,000, it's 1 in 17.

Source: Time, October 24, 2005

Four-year college grads make roughly $20,000 more than their high school trained counterparts. People with two-year degrees make only about $7,000 more a year than high school grads. The bottom line: A four-year degree is becoming America's most reliable elevator to a middle-class or higher standard of living.

Source: Business Week, October 31, 2005

Individuals with less than a ninth-grade education earn an estimated $976,350 over their lifetime. A high school dropout earns $1,150,968. A high school graduate earns $1,455,253. And a person with a bachelor's degree earns $2,567,174.

Source: Federal Reserve Bank of Dallas

It takes a staggering 83% of a poor family's annual income to fund the annual costs at private four-year colleges—up from 60% a decade ago.

Source: Business Week, October 31, 2005

Employers who hire young people right out of school and college professors who teach freshmen and sophomores said the public high school graduates they encounter had just "fair" or "poor" skills in:

- Grammar and spelling (73% of employers, 74% of college professors)
- Ability to write clearly (73% of employers, 75% of professors)
- Basic math (63% of employers, 65% of professors)

Source: Reality Check 2002

Employers and college professors also were not impressed with the attitudes high school graduates bring to the job or the classroom.

- Young people were given fair or poor ratings for "work habits, such as being organized and on time" by 69% of employers and 74% of professors.
- Students also were given low marks for "being motivated and conscientious" by 72% of employers and 58% of professors.

Source: Reality Check 2002

Within the next 10 years, 18 million jobs will require individuals with baccalaureate degrees. At the current level of incoming graduates to the workforce, we will have a shortfall of 6 million.

In 2000, 1.56 million U.S. residents ages 16 to 19 were not high school graduates AND not enrolled in school.

Source: Employment Policy Foundation

99% of all workers perform some reading-related work each day; to keep pace on the job they read 113 minutes a day.

50% of the U.S. population, ages 16-65, are functionally illiterate.

52% of high school graduates lack the basic skills required to do their jobs adequately; only 25% are considered to have excellent skills.

The U.S. ranks 49th among 156 countries in literacy.

Source: Adult Literacy Survey

The estimated yearly cost of illiteracy due to non-productivity, crime, and loss of tax revenue is $225 billion.

Source: Adult Literacy Survey

The healthcare industry estimates $73 billion per year of unnecessary healthcare expenses attributable to poor literacy. While the average American spent $5,440 for healthcare in 2002, the average healthcare cost for adults with low literacy skills was four times that amount, or $21,760. This may be due to the higher rate of hospitalization and the increased number of medication and treatment errors that they experience.

Source: Centers for Medicare & Medicaid Statistics, 2004;
Center for Health Care Strategies, Inc.
Health Literacy and Understanding Medical Information Fact Sheet

Latinos comprise 14% of the U.S. adult population and about half of this growing group (56%) goes online. By comparison, 71% of non-Hispanic whites and 60% of non-Hispanic blacks use the internet.

Source: pewinternet.org/pdfs/Latinos_Online_March_14_2007.pdf

Factor: The Growing Dependency Ratio

A dependency ratio is a measurement of the number of people working versus the number who need to be supported, including children and seniors. Working adults have always supported dependents; the majority of them have usually been children. Remarkably enough, the future dependency ratio is not going to change that drastically, although it will increase. The dependency ratio, which was around 20% in 1985, will start a major rise around 2015 when it hits 23.8%. By 2030, it will reach 35.5% according to the Social Security Administration. This is not that much higher than it was back in 1960, but back then it was children who were being supported. In the future, workers are going to be supporting aging adults, who are much, much more costly.

The costs of paying for future promised Social Security and Medicare health payouts to Baby Boomer retirees are estimated to amount to $250,000 per newborn. The demographic age wave that seemed so far off for so long is now upon us and threatens to swallow us: the oldest baby boomers will begin collecting Social Security benefits in 2008 and Medicare benefits in 2012. The burden of funding these entitlement programs falls on a declining number of workers. Back in 1950, the number of workers per Social Security beneficiary was 16.5. By 2000, the ratio had fallen to only 3.4. By 2030, there will only be two workers per retiree. In the meantime, the employment tax has risen fivefold. This means that the next generation may be faced with taxes that are nearly *twice* what we currently pay, to fund the benefits promised to the populous retiring generation.[6]

PLS Indicators: Stats, Facts, and Trends

Right now, it appears we are in the lull before the storm. The number of senior citizens has been steadily creeping higher, but the number of workers has been roughly keeping pace. This will change in 2008, when the first group of boomers, born in 1946, reach age 62—the age at which most people begin collecting Social Security benefits. Soon after, they will qualify for Medicare. At this point, the number of new workers entering the workforce will begin to decline, and the costs of funding the retirements of the Baby Boomer generation will soar.

A growing number of retirees must be supported by the production and income of relatively fewer workers. This is called the dependency ratio, or the ratio of the elderly population to that of the working age. Between now and 2080, the dependency ratio is expected to double.

In 1940, just a few years after the start of Social Security, only 54% of the population lived to 65 years old. The average remaining life expectancy for those surviving to age 65 was less than 13 years. Today, the percentage of men living to 65 is nearly 75%, and for women it is almost 85%. For those who live to age 65, men are expected to live almost another 16 years and women more than 20 years.

Source: Social Security Administration

The dependency ratio, which has hovered around 20% since 1985, ranging from a low of 20.6% in 2005 to a high of 21.6% in 1995, will start a major rise around 2015 when it hits 23.8%. By 2030 it will hit 35.5% and by 2080, it will reach an amazing 43.2%. While this is not significantly different than past dependency ratios (which are based on the proportion of workers compared to the total number of non-working children and retired seniors), the difference is that most of the dependents used to be children. In the future, most of the dependents will be adults, who are nearly ten times more expensive. In 1995, federal spending per child was $1,693 compared to $15,636 per senior citizen.

Source: Laurence Kotlikoff and Scott Burns, The Coming Generational Storm

More than 40% of the U.S. labor force will reach traditional retirement age by the end of the decade.

Source: Conference Board

In 1945, in the early days of the Social Security program, there were 41.9 contributing workers for every beneficiary. As the program and the elderly population grew, there was a huge decrease in the number of workers per beneficiary. By 1950, as a result, there were just 16.5 contributing workers for every beneficiary. The current ratio is 3.4 contributing workers for each beneficiary.

By 2040, under the intermediate projections of the Social Security Trustees, the ratio of beneficiaries to workers is projected to decline to 2 contributing workers for every beneficiary. These numbers reduce the issue to this: how will we afford to fund the retirements of a growing population and care for an aging population?

Source: Social Security Administration

Social Security has become a poor deal for workers. When the program started in 1935, the rate of return on a 40-year worker's investment was about 8%. Today, someone that age can expect a dismal 1%. Our children's rate of return will be negative if the program remains the same.

When the Social Security program was initiated in 1937, the average life expectancy in the U.S. was less than 65 years. Eligibility for benefits was set at age 65 in the expectation that fewer than half of the workers would collect Social Security (because they wouldn't live long enough). Furthermore, when the program started, there were a lot of workers paying into the program and few receiving benefits.

Source: Social Security: A Tale of Two Problems, Washington Policy Center

Under current census projections, the number of working-age Americans (ages 18 to 64) to each resident 65 years and up will fall from 4.8 in the year 2000 to 2.7 in 2050. Maintaining even a modestly positive actuarial ratio of 4 to 1 would require dramatically increasing U.S. population growth to 607 million by 2050, compared to the 392 million now projected. With the fertility of most native-born Americans well under replacement levels, achieving such rapid growth in so short a time would require massive increases in already high levels of direct immigration boosted by the higher birthrates of the foreign born.

Source: Social Security: A Tale of Two Problems, Washington Policy Center

Americans are living longer and having fewer children, and this alters the ratio between the number of workers and retirees. In 1937, 42 workers paid 2% in payroll tax to support every retiree. In 1950, 16 workers paid 3% in tax for each retiree. Today, around 3.3 workers pay 12.4% in payroll tax for each retiree. By 2025, there will be two workers per retiree and by 2050, 1.3 workers per retiree.

Source: Social Security: A Tale of Two Problems, Washington Policy Center

Factor: Women in the Workplace

Women now account for nearly half of all American workers; their representation has almost doubled in the past half-century, from 33.9% of women working in 1950 to nearly 60% working today.[7] Were it not for the increased workforce participation rates of women, the labor storm forecast would be even more dire and the Social Security crisis would be even more urgent.

The statistics regarding women and employment are impressive. According to the *Monthly Labor Review*, nearly 60% of mothers of infants are in the labor force. Seventy-three percent of mothers with older children work, although only about half work full time. The average family under age sixty in the United States now has two earners. Given these facts, it is unlikely that women's workplace participation can increase much more than it already has; women's labor force participation rates are not expected to be high enough to offset the decline in the men's participation rate in the future.

Unfortunately, the rise in the number of working women has coincided with a decline in the number of working men from 86.4% in 1950 to 74.9% today. Perhaps the fact that more men have working wives has allowed them to feel financially able to become stay-at-home dads, or to retire early. The largest declines, according to MIT economist Laurence Kotlikoff, have been among men 55 and over. For them, the employment rate has fallen nearly 20% since 1950. Men over 65 have left the workforce in even greater numbers: in 1950, 45.8% worked, but in 1998, only 16.5% did.[8]

A corresponding factor behind the increased labor participation rates of women is their phenomenal educational success, at both the college and graduate levels. With increased levels of education, women now enjoy higher economic value in the workplace. Unfortunately, male degree completion rates are in decline, so the gains have come with corresponding losses. Also, increased labor participation rates of women have their own cost. Working women have fewer children, and declining birth rates are, themselves, the major force behind the coming Perfect Labor Storm. The fact is, the higher a woman's educational level, the fewer children she is likely to have. This merely compounds the labor crisis of the future.

The following chart depicts the changes in female and male labor participation rates from 1950 through what is projected by the year 2050.

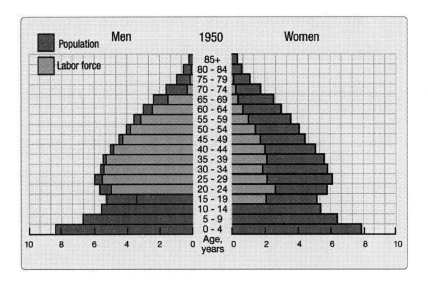

In 1950, our population still resembled a pyramid when sorted by age, with large numbers of children and youth and few elderly. Very few men between the ages of 20 and 65 were not in the workforce.

On the next chart, it is easy to notice the dramatic increase in the labor participation rate by women. However, do not overlook the corresponding *decline* in the male labor force participation rate, which begins to become quite noticeable in the 55-59 year old age group. Also, notice the flattening of the demographic pyramid into more of a rectangle, representing increased longevity and decreased birthrates.

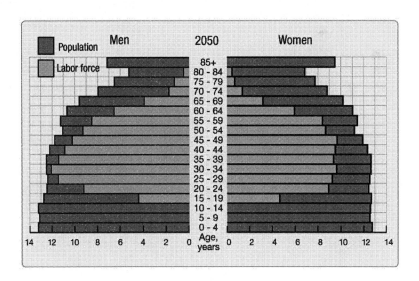

PLS Indicators: Stats, Facts, and Trends

Women experienced nearly all of the net employment growth for better jobs between 2000 and 2005. Women accounted for 1.7 million of the 1.9 million jobs paying above the median age during that period. Women represented all of the employment growth among management, business, and financial occupations, and most of the increase for professional occupations. Much of the employment increase below the median wage occurred in construction and extraction occupations and in low-wage food preparation and serving-related occupations.

Source: Bureau of Labor Statistics

Highest-Paid Occupations for Women (2005 weekly earnings)

Pharmacists	$1,483
Chief executives	$1,413
Lawyers	$1,354
Computer software engineers	$1,174
Physicians and surgeons	$1,134

Source: U.S. Department of Labor Women's Bureau

In 1950, 1 in 3 women participated in the workforce. By 1998, 3 of every 5 women of working age were in the workforce.

In 1950, the labor participation rate for women was only 34%, compared to 60% in 1998. Today, the current participation rate for women aged 25-64 exceeds 76%.

Source: Bureau of Labor Statistics

Nearly 100,000 women, half of all the women in the active U.S. armed forces, are mothers. Another 200,000 women serve in the National Guard, Air Force and Army Reserve. 83% of centenarians are women. The number of women age 100 or older will double by 2010.

Source: Agelight

26.7 million women ages 15 to 44 are childless, which is 44% of the women in that age group. In 1990, 24.3 million women ages 15 to 44 were childless.

Percentage of women who worked during pregnancy:

      1961-65: 44.4%   1991-95: 66.8%

Percentage of women who returned to work within six months after having their first child:

      1961-65: 13.7%   1991-95: 52.3%

Percentage of women who worked during pregnancy and then quit their job:

      1961-65: 62.8%   1991-95: 26.9%

Percentage of women who worked while pregnant between 1991-95:

Bachelor's degree or more:	87.1%
High school graduate:	60.2%
Less than high school graduate:	28.6%

Source: U.S. Census Bureau

Women's labor force participation, a low 33.9% in 1950, increased significantly during the 1970s and 1980s and reached 57.5% in 1990. In 1999, the women's participation rate reached a peak of 60%.

By 2000, however, the rate had declined slightly to 59.9%, and since then, it has been displaying a pattern of slow decline in each successive period, falling to 59.3% in 2005. The participation rate of women is projected to be 59.4% in 2020 and 55.1% in 2050. Women's participation rate is expected to remain below the men's rate through 2050.

Source: Monthly Labor Review

Between 1950 and 1999 the number of people in the labor force grew from 62.2 million to 139.4 million, an increase of 77.2 million. Of that number, women were 46.5 million or 60%.

Source: Labor Force by Sex and Age, 1950 to 2025

The proportion of bachelor's degrees awarded to women reached a post-war high in 2003 at an estimated 57%.

Source: Employment Policy Foundation

There are 10.4 million women business owners in the U.S., and women-owned businesses generate nearly $2.3 trillion in annual revenues.

Approximately 50% of privately held, women-owned firms in the top 50 metropolitan areas collectively employ 9.5 million people and generate $1.3 trillion in annual sales.

Among privately held companies in the U.S., 48% are at least half-owned by women, an increase from 44% in 1997, according to the Center for Women's Business Research. The reasons these entrepreneurs cited for starting their own businesses included the freedom to set their own schedules, the chance to pursue an opportunity, and the desire to escape from the "glass ceiling" that they felt limited their careers in corporations.

Source: Center for Women's Business Research

By 2030, women will hold a larger share of management and professional jobs than men.

Source: Employment Policy Foundation

The labor participation rate of men has been continually decreasing, having registered 76.4% in 1990, 74.8% in 2000, and 73.3% in 2005. The rate is projected to be 70.0% in 2020 and 66.0% in 2050.

Source: Monthly Labor Review

Factor: Presenteeism, Not Just Absenteeism

Declining numbers of skilled workers proportionate to the number of available jobs are a demographic fact. Many employers seek to counteract this reality by trying to squeeze more and more work out of fewer employees, but the ability to increase individual productivity has a limit. The average American worker is already struggling to keep up with the current demands and suffering significant stress. Increasing productivity further will be difficult.

The idea that technology will enable fewer employees to produce more and more is certainly appealing, but fraught with potential challenges. The reality is that increased productivity demands are likely to increase worker stress, which will invariably show up in increased absenteeism, healthcare costs, or voluntary turnover.

More and more employees are stressed on the job, resulting in absenteeism, m istakes, accidents, and job-related illnesses. When employees are overworked, they are apt to bring decreased motivational levels and increased healthcare costs to the organization. In a seller's job market, stressed-out, overworked employees may simply leave, since finding a new position will not be hard. This results in recruitment and retraining costs, if replacements can even be found.

Equally likely, workers will simply "check out" motivationally, attending work to collect a paycheck without contributing much. They will keep their chairs warm and be physically present, but they will not produce much. Such "presenteeism," which has also been called "warm-chair attrition," is liable to continue to be a costly factor of business life for managers unable to motivate and engage their employees.

PLS Indicators: Stats, Facts, and Trends

The productivity research challenge of the new millennium is the measurement of "presenteeism"… employees who are at the work site regularly, but for a variety of reasons, are not producing as they should.

Source: The Health Promotion Research Advocate (HERO) Vol. 1, No. 1, 1998

Presenteeism signifies that a number of employees, even those with perfect attendance records on the job, are nonetheless working with impairments and disabilities, causing them to work less efficiently, resulting in employers losing as much as 32 times more productivity from presenteeism as from absenteeism.

Source: Clark A. Marcus, Work/Life article

Presenteeism reportedly accounts for 80% of lost productivity.

Source: American Productivity Audit

The cost of presenteeism: If a company is comprised of 1000 workers, each worker is expected to work 2000 hours (50 weeks x 40 hours) minus any overtime; ideally the workforce could gauge productivity to 2 million hours. If every worker loses 115 hours to presenteeism, then 115,000 productive hours are lost—a reduction of almost 6%. Assume that the productivity capacity of a worker is 4 times his/her fully loaded salary. If salary is $50,000, then productivity is $100 per hour. ($50,000/50 weeks = $1000/40 hours = $25 per hour x 4 = $100). Therefore, $100 x 115,000 presenteeism hours = $11,500,000 dollars of lost productivity. Said another way, the financial loss of presenteeism in this example is equal to the salaries of 230 workers.

Source: American Journal of Health Promotion (Vol. 4, No. 2), June/July, 2001

The 2006 CCH Unscheduled Absence Survey found that the rate of unscheduled absenteeism climbed to its highest level since 1999, costing some large employers an estimated $850,000 per year in direct payroll costs, and even more when lost productivity, morale, and temporary labor costs are considered.

The 2006 CCH Unscheduled Absence Survey also found that personal illness accounts for only 35% of unscheduled absences, while 65% of absences are due to other reasons, including family issues (24%), personal needs (18%), stress (12%) and entitlement mentality (11%).

Besides loyalty (36%) and too much work (66%), what are the other causes of presenteeism?

- Lack of coverage for the sick employee's workload: 56%
- Don't want to use vacation time: 50%
- Saving sick time for future use: 41%
- Fear of discipline: 46%

Source: 2006 CCH Unscheduled Absence Survey

Healthcare expenses associated with absenteeism can run upward of $74 billion annually for U.S. companies. Researchers derived this figure by taking into account spillover expenses, such as overtime and overstaffing, that companies incur to compensate for the absence of a worker.

Source: "How to Present the Business Case for Healthcare Quality to Employers,"
Mark Pauly, co-author of the study

On any given day, 6.4% of manufacturing employees miss a day's work. A survey from Circadian Technologies shows that unscheduled absences cost companies $3,600 per hourly employee per year and $2,650 per salaried employee each year. And that doesn't take into account the costs associated with "presenteeism," defined as showing up for work when one is sick or distracted by family turmoil, resulting in a sub-par effort. In a manufacturing environment, presenteeism can lead to manufacturing defects or on-the-job injuries that can drive up a company's cost of doing business.

Source: The Manufacturer, www.manufacturer.com

A new study from the MetLife Mature Market Institute® (MMI) reports that the cost to U.S. business due to lost productivity of working caregivers is $17.1 billion to $33.6 billion per year.

According to The MetLife Caregiving Costs Study: Productivity Losses to U.S. Business, produced in conjunction with the National Alliance for Caregiving (NAC), the average caregiver costs an employer $2,110 per year. For those caregivers providing the most intense levels of care, the cost per employee is $2,441, totaling $17.1 billion. The total annual cost for all caregivers is $33.6 billion.

In addition to the study's main findings, the MMI also reports that for all levels of caregivers:

- Of the 2.4% of employees who leave the workforce entirely to be caregivers (200,000 men and 184,000 women), the cost to replace them is $6.6 billion.
- Absenteeism, reported by the majority of caregiving employees, costs $5 billion, while partial absenteeism, affecting virtually all working caregivers, accounts for nearly $2 billion in losses.
- Workday interruptions, at least one hour per week per caregiver, cost $6.3 billion.
- Having a crisis that requires attention during the workday is experienced by 60% of employed caregivers and costs $3.8 billion.
- Other lost productivity costs include: costs for supervision ($1.8 billion), costs associated with unpaid leave ($3.4 billion) and those resulting in a reduction from full to part-time status ($4.8 billion).

Source: The entire version of "The MetLife Caregiving Costs Study:
Productivity Losses to U.S. Business" can be found at: www.maturemarketinstitute.com

Executives alone cost American industry more than $10 billion annually through lost workdays, hospitalization, and early death by stress. This does not include the results of other signs of stress, such as mistakes, slower response time, and loss of concentration.

Employees' diminished capacity on the job is costing U.S. employers about $250 billion a year.

Source: Advance PCS Inc.

Lost productivity due to presenteeism was, on average, 7.5 times greater than productivity lost to absenteeism. In some cases, the ratio was 15:1, 20:1, or even approached 30:1.

Source: The Health Coalition of Tampa, Florida (1999)

Chronic pain among the nation's workforce rose nearly 40% between 1996 and 2006 according to a national survey of 1,103 full-time U.S. workers and 251 employment benefits managers.

- 89% of full-time employees with chronic pain experienced pain at work.
- 89% of full-time employees with chronic pain typically go to work instead of staying home when in pain.
- 27% more employees missed work five or more days because of chronic pain during 2006 vs. in 1996.
- 46% of employees with chronic pain said the pain often or sometimes affects their ability to perform their job.
- 65% of employers surveyed cited pain-related conditions as a cause of lost productivity.
- $1.1 billion of lost wages in 2006 was attributable to employees calling in sick due to any pain-related condition.

Source: National Pain Foundation (2007)

Labor Forecasts by Industry

Of course, labor forecasts vary depending on the specific field or industry. Certain fields that are in particularly high demand or that require skilled and technically proficient workers are going to face more critical shortages than others. In anticipation of these shortages, the U.S. Department of Labor has designated certain fields as being "High Growth." This means that the field is economically critical, projected to add substantial numbers of new jobs, and being transformed by technology and innovation. These industries include Advanced Manufacturing, Aerospace, Automotive, Biotechnology, Construction, Energy, Financial Services, Geospatial Technology, Health Care, Homeland Security, Hospitality, Information Technology , NanoTechnology, Retail, and Transportation. These "High Growth" Industries fall under general job families. Of course, the workplace is changing so rapidly these days that entirely new careers are being created.

New "New" Careers

The United States may keep shedding jobs to foreign countries, but it cranks out new occupations like no one else. In fact, many jobs that don't even exist yet will be the hot new jobs by the time this year's college freshmen graduate. Here are just five of the hottest jobs you can get into now, according to a survey by Business 2.0:

> Disease Mapper
> Robot Programmer
> Information Engineer
> Radiosurgeon
> Second Life Lawyer

Now let's take a look at some of the jobs that are going to be especially difficult to fill during the coming Labor Storm:

Healthcare

Nowhere are the projected future labor shortages destined to have more impact than in the field of healthcare. Aging Baby Boomers will increase the demand for healthcare services just as the pool of available healthcare workers simultaneously dwindles. Our aging population is already increasing the number of inpatient admissions and outpatient procedures nationwide.

The health care industry, including general and specialty practices, hospitals and other service organizations are confronted with vacancies, some as high as 50%. According to the *Atlanta Business Chronicle,* the U.S. Department of Health and Human Services reported that nursing homes currently need 181,000 to 310,000 nurse aides to reach full staff levels.

Technical advances in the field of lifesciences are increasing the need for highly skilled workers and technicians, but they are not being produced quickly enough. Already, hospital administrators are reporting significant shortages of registered nurses, radiology technicians, pharmacists, laboratory technicians and licensed practical nurses.[9] Many hospitals are having to resort to hiring expensive temporary help to fill gaps. As expected, the demand for home health aides is also increasing.

Health care has been designated as a "High Growth Industry" by the U.S. Department of Labor, with the following "In-Demand" jobs expected to grow faster than average and to face the most severe labor shortages within the next 5-7 years.

Forecast through 2014 for Highest-Demand Jobs:

	Number of jobs	Percentage growth
Registered Nurses	3,096,100	29%
Nursing Aides, Orderlies	1,780,600	22%
Home Health Aides:	973,700	56%
Personal Care Aides	988,500	41%
Licensed Practical Nurses	850,000	17%
Medical Assistants:	586,000	52%
Medical Secretaries	436,500	17%
Health Service Managers	304,700	23%
Pharmacists/Pharmacy Techs	286,600	25%

Dental Assistants/Hygienists	271,000	43%
Physical Therapists	211,300	37%
Medical Records Personnel	204,700	29%
Medical Lab Technologists	187,800	21%
Medical Lab Technicians	183,300	25%
Rehabilitation Counselors	162,000	24%
Respiratory Therapists	120,300	28%

Source: Bureau of Labor Statistics

Information Technology

The field of Information Technology is also designated as a "High Growth Industry" by the Department of Labor. Skilled technicians will continue to be in high demand. Many Information Technology jobs in the United States continue to remain unfilled due to an ongoing lack of qualified applicants. The United States currently has a national IT workforce of 10.4 million, but over 450,000 vacancies went unfilled in 2001 because of the "Talent Gap"—a shortfall of workers with required skills—according to a report issued by the Information Technology Association of America (ITAA.)

The skilled labor shortage in IT has already resulted in large-scale hiring of foreign workers to overcome shortages of American skilled workers. The ITAA report goes on to point out that Information Technology employment remains at the forefront of the U.S. economy, and accounts for 7% of the nation's workforce. It is interesting to note that most Information Technology workers are employed by non-IT firms.

Forecast through 2014 for Highest-Demand Jobs:

	Number of jobs	Percentage growth
Software Engineers/Applications	682,2000	48%
Computer Systems Analysts	639,500	31%
Computer Support Specialists	637,600	23%
Software Engineers/Software Systems	486,500	43%
Network Systems Analysts	357,500	55%
Computer Systems Administrators	385,200	38%
Computer Programmers	464,300	2%
Database Administrators	144,300	38%

Source: Bureau of Labor Statistics

Business and Retail

Competition for qualified retail workers will intensify in the coming labor storm, as will efforts to reduce turnover by improving retention statistics. The demand for employees in business and financial operations will remain strong, with particularly high demand expected for accountants, computer support, and personal financial planners. Cam Marston predicts that employees with "soft skills," including customer service, sales, marketing and interpersonal skills, will be in particularly short supply, since these core skills are not being taught at home as they were in the past.[10] As Baby Boomers age, they will need assistance with managing their finances, so demand for personal financial advisors is expected to increase. The fields expected to grow faster than average include.

Forecast through 2014 for Highest-Demand Jobs:

	Number of jobs	Percentage growth
Retail Salespersons	4,991,900	17%
Customer Service Representatives	2,534,200	23%
Executive Secretary/Admin. Assistant	1,739,300	12%
Accountants and Auditors	1,440,100	22%
Sales Representatives	569,000	14%
Billing Agents	540,800	3%
Sales Managers	402,700	20%
Marketing Managers	227,700	21%
Personal Financial Advisors	199,000	26%
Compensation/Benefits Managers	69,800	21%

Source: Bureau of Labor Statistics

Hospitality

Labor shortages in the Hospitality field are already in critical ranges. Designated a "High Growth" field, the U.S. Department of Labor invested more than $2 million in 2005 to address the workforce needs of the Hospitality industry by identifying the industry's hiring, training, and retention challenges and coming up with workable solutions. The problems center around an insufficient pipeline of new workers, high turnover, lack of English proficiency, deficient "soft skills" in this customer-service-oriented field, and lack of consistent training or skills certifications. The hiring challenges within this industry will remain formidable in the foreseeable future.

Forecast through 2014 for Highest-Demand Jobs:

	Number of jobs	Percentage growth
Waiters and Waitresses	2,627,400	17%
Maids	1,587,400	12%
Food Preparation	1,063,700	20%
Counter Attendants	545,900	15%
Bartenders	544,700	15%
Dining Room Attendants	464,000	16%
Food Service Managers	414,100	12%
Cooks, Short Order Cooks	257,300	12%
Hotel and Resort Desk Clerks	228,900	17%
Hosts and Hostesses	157,000	6%
Chefs and Head Cooks	145,700	17%

Source: Bureau of Labor Statistics

Social Services and Education

One field that is going to experience a particularly serious demographic turnover is Education, both K-12 and postsecondary. Schools and colleges nationwide will soon face a mass exodus of the majority of their workforce, as tenured Baby Boomers retire. According to the National Education Association, more than a million veteran teachers are nearing retirement, and we will need more than two million new teachers in the next decade.

The statistics for turnover among new teachers are shocking: nearly 50% of teachers leave the profession within five years. Two-thirds of the nation's mathematics and science teaching force will retire by 2010. Forty percent of the current public school teaching force does not plan to be teaching five years from now, and the K-12 teaching force is aging rapidly. The proportion of K-12 teachers who are 50 years of age and older has risen from one in four (24%) in 1996 to 42% in 2005. Nearly three quarters of a million K-12 teachers will retire by 2010. That is nearly 30% of the entire teaching force! Likewise, Social Service agencies will struggle to fill vacancies with qualified applicants during the coming labor shortage.

Forecast through 2014 for Highest-Demand Jobs:

	Number of jobs	Percentage growth
Postsecondary Teachers	2,152,600	32%
Elementary school Teachers	1,922,200	18%
Secondary school Teachers	1,172,200	14%
Teacher Assistants	1,478,200	14%
Middle School Teachers	714,100	14%
Special Education Teachers (K-12)	534,100	23%
Mental Health Counselor	269,000	27%
School Administrators (K-12)	249,000	10%
Community Service Manager	168,500	26%
College Administrators	159,800	21%
Preschool/Childcare Administrators	74,700	28%

Source: Bureau of Labor Statistics

Management

The management ranks of American businesses are already stretched very thin, and leaner organizations have been trying to get more done with fewer people for decades. No relief is in sight, as the demand for management workers is expected to grow faster than average during the coming decade.

Because management positions tend to require seasoned personnel, it is often best to develop new talent from within. But because of labor shortages, it will become increasingly difficult to keep high performers from being lured away by other firms. The primary focus, therefore, should be on retention of management personnel, since we may soon see a return to the days of signing bonuses and other premium hiring incentives. During the coming labor shortage, organizations need to pay extra-special attention to the satisfaction levels of their valued managers and employees. Competitors and headhunters certainly will be doing whatever they can to lure top talent regardless of the source.

Forecast through 2014 for Highest-Demand Jobs:

	Number of jobs	Percentage growth
Financial Managers	606,300	15%
Training and Development Specialists	260,800	21%
First-line supervisors/Personal service	243,700	18%
Employment/Recruitment Specialists	237,400	30%
Marketing Managers	227,700	21%
Human Resources Assistant	200,200	17%
Compensation/Benefits Managers	188,800	21%
Public Relations Manager	70,000	22%
Training and Development Managers	47,000	26%

Source: Bureau of Labor Statistics

Sales

As Thomas Watson, the founder of IBM, wisely pointed out, "Nothing happens until somebody sells something." Likewise, managing customer relations throughout the selling process is essential to sales completion and fulfillment, and customer services representatives are going to be in particularly high demand during the coming years. According to Marston, "People with sales skills will become more important and harder to find. Many employers have expressed their disappointment when, upon hiring a Gen Xer or a New Millennial, they learn that these two generations are extremely fearful of rejection and, after being told 'no' by several customers, leave their jobs (or quit trying and stay, which is worse than leaving.)"[11] Finding replacement employees with the proper attitudinal composition for sales will be harder than ever, considering the characteristics of younger "potential" employees. Across the board, steady, consistent growth and demand for sales professionals will remain an ongoing challenge for firms requiring these services during the future labor shortage.

Forecast through 2014 for Highest-Demand Jobs:

	Number of jobs	Percentage growth
Customer Service Representatives	2,534,200	23%
Sales Representatives (non-technical)	1,641,100	13%
Customer Support Specialists	637,600	23%
Driver/Sales Workers	513,400	14%
Sales Representatives, Technical	454,500	14%
Sales Managers	402,000	20%
Securities Sales Agents	313,000	12%
Advertising Sales Agents	179,600	16%
Demonstrators and Product Promoters	137,500	16%

Source: Bureau of Labor Statistics

Construction

As we've seen during recent housing booms and busts, the housing industry has the power to influence the economy at large, including the stock market. Without adequate numbers of construction workers to fuel this important industry, the housing sector is liable to stagnate. Already, housing relies heavily upon immigrant laborers to fill vacant positions. This shortfall is only going to increase as the demographic pool of young workers declines, and the repercussions of this anticipated slowdown will be widespread.

Forecast through 2014 for Highest-Demand Jobs:

	Number of jobs	Percentage growth
Carpenters	1,534,600	14%
Maintenance and Repair Workers	1,533,500	15%
Electricians	733,700	12%
Plumbers and Pipefitters	576,600	16%
Construction Managers	475,300	10%
Cement Masons	232,800	16%
Roofers	188,800	17%
Brickmasons	173,700	12%
Iron and Steel Workers	83,400	15%
Helpers, Brick and Stone Masons	71,400	15%

Source: Bureau of Labor Statistics

Transportation

Increasingly, the speed of commerce depends on the speed of transportation. Steve Russell, CEO of a major trucking firm, foresees a "capacity shortage, largely the result of an overall shortage of competent drivers." He sees this as being due to demographic characteristics of the industry, specifically an "aging driver population not being replaced by young people" and "the industry is anticipating that we are likely to face an almost alarming shortage of drivers in the years ahead." Russell also points to the problems of incredibly high turnover among truck drivers, which averages approximately 125% among large fleets.[12] Other sectors of the transportation industry are also likely to be hard-hit by labor shortages. Demand for public and mass transportation services is liable to increase in coming years as older people will be less capable of driving independently.

Forecast through 2014 for Highest-Demand Jobs:

	Number of jobs	Percentage growth
Freight and Material Movers	2,678,300	10%
Truck Drivers	1,961,800	13%
Packers and Packagers	965,600	10%
Bus drivers, School	526,100	14%
Bus drivers (Transit and Intercity)	231,300	22%
Automotive Repair	221,200	10%
Flight Attendants	119,200	16%
Railroad Conductors and Yardmasters	45,100	20%
Transportation Attendants	32,000	16%
Transportation Inspectors	28,500	11%
Subway and Streetcar Operators	10,400	14%

Source: Bureau of Labor Statistics

Manufacturing

Much has already been written about the decline of the American manufacturing sector and the coming labor shortage will only exacerbate the situation. With cheap labor to be found overseas, outsourcing is being touted as the solution to America's limited labor pool and preservation of competitive advantage. However, loss of manufacturing potential places America in a possible strategic and economic disadvantage. Anticipated job growth will be highest among engineering departments, but labor shortfalls will be widespread throughout the manufacturing sector.

Forecast through 2014 for Highest-Demand Jobs:

	Number of jobs	Percentage growth
Supervisors-Production Workers	750,300	3%
Helpers-Production Workers	521,800	8%
Production and Expediting Clerks	314,500	8%
Mechanical Engineers	251,000	11%
Industrial Engineers	205,000	16%
Electrical Engineers	174,300	12%
Industrial Production Managers	161,600	1%
Industrial Engineering Technicians	76,000	10%
Chemical Engineers	33,900	11%

Source: Bureau of Labor Statistics

Where the Hiring Competition Will Be Most Fierce

Top 25 Occupations with the Most Openings through 2014
Requirement: On-the-Job Training

Retail salesperson
Cashiers
Waiters and waitresses
Food preparation and servers, including fast food
Freight, stock and material movers
Office clerks
Janitors and cleaners
Customer Service representatives
Stock clerks and order fillers
Sales representatives (non-technical)
Child care workers
Receptionists and information clerks
Truck drivers
Executive secretaries and administrative assistants
Landscaping and groundskeeping workers
Maids and housekeeping workers
Maintenance and repair workers
First-line supervisors of office workers
Teacher assistants
Home health aides
Team assemblers
Carpenters
Personal and home care aides
Counter attendants (food service)
Cooks, restaurant

Source: Bureau of Labor Statistics

Top 25 Occupations with the Most Openings through 2014
Requirement: Postsecondary Training

Registered nurses
Nursing aides, orderlies, and attendants
Automotive service technicians and mechanics
Licensed practical nurses
Hairdressers and cosmetologists
Preschool teachers
Computer support specialists
Medical secretaries
Real estate sales agents
Bus and truck mechanics
Fitness trainers
Legal secretaries
Paralegals and legal assistants
Dental hygienists
Medical and clinical laboratory technicians
Radiologic technologists
EMT/paramedic
Medical records and health information technicians
Library technicians
Respiratory therapists
Electrical engineering technicians
Gaming dealers
Appraisers and assessors of real estate
Aircraft mechanics and service technicians
Medical transcriptionists

Source: Bureau of Labor Statistics

Top 25 Occupations with the Most Openings through 2014

Requirement: Bachelor's degree or above

Postsecondary teachers

General and operations managers

Elementary school teachers

Accountants and auditors

Secondary school teachers

Computer software engineers

Middle school teachers

Physicians and surgeons

Computer systems analysts

Lawyers

Management analysts

Computer software engineers

Financial managers

Network systems and data communications analysts

Chief executives

Clergy

Network and computer systems administrators

Sales managers

Computer and information systems managers

Property, real estate, and community association managers

Construction managers

Insurance sales agents

Computer programmers

Medical and health services managers

Pharmacists

Source: Bureau of Labor Statistics

More Storm Clouds Forming:

Intergenerational Conflict in the Workplace

One association manager, Laura, summed up the universal problem facing most organizations this way: "We've got a problem: the average age of our membership is in the 50s. Our board of directors consists of members in their 60s and 70s. We're losing young members left and right. Our association is on a collision course between the old farts and spoiled rotten brats."

No one ever described the generation gap quite that way before, but Laura was right. Her association, like so many organizations and businesses, is on a collision course.

"Most organizations have found themselves in a quandary," say generation gurus Carolyn Martin and Bruce Tulgan in their published report, *Managing the Generation Mix.*[13] "They've finally figured out how to recruit young talent, only to watch them clash with older, seasoned employees over issues like work ethic, respect for authority, dress codes, and every work arrangement imaginable. And they're not sure what to do about it."

Generational clashes have been around for ages. Each generation has viewed the next with skepticism and cynicism, saying essentially, that "kid's today just don't have the same work ethic." For the past decade, all we heard about was the poor work ethic of Generation X. That is, until Generation Y or the Millennials arrived on the scene. Ironically, in a twist of fate, one of the most common conflicts arising in the workplace today is the result of the Xer's complaining about the work ethic of the Millennials!

Yes, that is true. In a landmark Center for Applied Research study of the Millennial Generation released last year, two responses dominated:

1. The Millennials are spoiled rotten brats whose parents have given them everything.
2. The Millennials are extremely talented and will bring the most advanced technology and teamwork skills to the workforce.

What if both sides are correct and the Millennials are spoiled, narcissistic brats who possess the talent and skills businesses need?

While that scenario may cause your heart to skip a beat, make your skin crawl, and send chills up and down your spine, GET OVER IT! The Millennials are, and will be, for the next two decades, the replacement workforce every manager has been clamoring for. Blame it on the Boomers who lowered our birthrate to historic lows. Blame it on society who raised a generation of latch-key children and then expected them to play ball with the rest of the kids. Blame it on the helicopter parents who won't let go of their kids long after they reach adulthood. Blame it on immigration policy. Blame it on whomever and whatever you want. The fact remains the Millennials are the replacement workers you've been waiting for.

No one debates that each generation is different. But different doesn't mean bad—just different. What Laura and her association members were experiencing was a clash of generations: the old farts, Traditionals and Boomers, pitted against the spoiled rotten brats, the Gen Xers and Millennials.

Once upon a time, older employees of a certain age were expected to leave the workplace to make room for upcoming, younger workers. Typically, no more than two distinct generations (the older, management generation and the younger, emerging workers) shared the workplace at any one time.

No more. Because of skilled labor shortages, which are going to reach "Perfect Labor Storm Category 5" levels in the near future, American businesses are going to need to hold on to as many workers of every age as possible.

As a result of efforts to retain aging workers longer, and to fill the new jobs being created as well as replace retiring workers, the workforce is becoming much more multigenerational. Today, we have four distinct generations sharing the workplace: the "Traditional" older workers, the Baby Boomers, Generation X, and Generation Y (also called the "Millennials" or the "Net" generation). This means that the workplace will be increasingly characterized not just by an aging workforce, but also by *increased age diversity*.

This generational "crowding" is making for some major conflict and miscommunication in the workplace. That's because each generation has its own distinct set of values, shaped by their unique social conditions, political events, economic conditions, major crises and childhood experiences. Each generation also *reacts* to the generation before them, and this reaction becomes part of its own identity and defining characteristics. These differences can lead to major misunderstandings between coworkers raised in different eras.

Authors Warren Bennis and Robert Thomas have their own unique view of this situation. They see the generation gap as being between what they call the "geeks" (the younger, "digital" generations) and the "geezers" (the older, "analog" generations). The analog world in which today's older generations grew up was primarily linear. It rewarded specialization and experience, followed a mechanical understanding of the world, and favored organizational hierarchy. The digital world of the younger generations is nonlinear; it favors a flat organizational structure and rewards the generalist with the beginner's mind. Rather than a mechanical view of the world, it favors a more fluid and changing "living systems" model.[14] This is a major paradigm shift that increasingly divides different generations in the workplace.

According to a survey by Lee Hecht Harrison, more than 60% of employers say they are experiencing tension between employees from different generations. The older generation has always complained about the younger one, but in the modern workplace the misunderstanding works both ways. Today, you might have a fresh college graduate managing a person thirty, or even forty years older! It can be difficult on both sides to handle the disparities of this reality. Managing this conflict, and finding ways to value the unique contributions made by these four unique generations in the workforce will be a challenge for all businesses in the future.

The different social conditions that defined each generation also equipped them with very predictable approaches that govern how they respond to challenges which mean that each generation also has unique strengths to offer. The goal of management is to maximize the strengths of these different generations while minimizing conflict. How well the organization manages this intergenerational cooperation is going to affect retention rates and competitiveness.

According to generational gurus Dr. Carolyn Martin and Bruce Tulgan who have written extensively about intergenerational conflict in the workplace in *Managing the Generation Mix: From Collision to Collaboration*, as well as *Managing the Generation Mix 2007*, these different, distinct generations currently occupy the current proportions of the workforce:

TOTAL WORKFORCE POPULATION: 150 million (EST.)

	PERCENTAGE
Traditional ("Silent") Generation (born before 1946)	6.5%
Baby Boomers (1946-64)	41.5%
Generation X (1965-77)	29.5%
Generation Y (born 1978-1990)	22.5% [15]

Notice that while Generations X and Y make up the majority of the workplace, the Baby Boomers still comprise over 40% and currently are the single generation with the greatest representation. As Boomers begin to leave the workforce and members of Generation Y, Z and beyond begin to fill those vacancies, the pool of talent from which employers draw is going to change dramatically. take a look at the four generations currently sharing the American workplace:

TRADITIONALS OR THE "SILENT" GENERATION (born before 1946)

Prepare to say goodbye to the Traditional workers, whose core values includ dedication, adherence to rules, hard work, patience, delayed reward, conformity, duty before pleasure, and loyalty. Now comprising less than 7% of the employed population, this generation won't be in the workforce much longer.

The Traditional generation thrived within traditional, hierarchical organizations. Members of this generation did not seek to change the system, but rather to work within it. Growing up in large families with many siblings, they often stayed in the same hometown for their lifetime. They also expected to stay with one employer for an entire career. Their childhoods were characterized by spending many hours each day with a stay-at-home parent, and they grew up viewing the world as "safe" and stable. They were raised to believe in traditional institutions like school, the government, and the church. This faith extended to the organizations that hired them.

According to Martin and Tulgan, Traditionals were raised to follow rules, established procedures and to listen to authority. They generally enjoy belonging to organizations, and appreciate the sense of security and affiliation they provide. In fact, when they weren't working in a large corporation, Traditionals were prone to joining organization in their leisure time. Groups such as Kiwanis, Rotary, and the Masons now face the crisis of aging memberships; younger generations have less interest in joining their ranks. Pearl Harbor, a defining experience, forever marked this generation with a military imprint.

Bennis and Thomas refer to the coming-of-age years of this generation as the "era of limits." Characterized by the Cold War, these were the years in which Big Business flourished, and employee benefits were born. The ideas of reciprocal loyalty between employer and employee and the "organization man" characterized this time period. Rather than two-career families, this generation knew the two-person career, in which the stay-at-home spouse was expected to facilitate her husband's corporate advancement by handling everything on the homefront. Douglas McGregor's paternalistic "Theory X" management style prevailed, as did military styles of leadership.

While the stability of the Traditionals may be viewed by organizations as a positive trait, younger workers may see this generation as resisting change and being unwilling to adapt. Traditional employees tend to be process-oriented, meaning they are accustomed to following procedures. They also possess a strong work ethic. They generally don't like taking risks and prefer stability.

Traditionals may be the last generation who believed implicitly in lifetime employer-employee loyalty. That implied bond was broken with the downsizing trend of the late 1980s, which changed the way younger generations view their relationship to an employer.

Traditional employees have a hard time understanding the job-hopping mentality of younger workers, believing that loyalty to an employer and sacrifice are prime virtues. Some Traditionals may harbor the age-old expectation that younger generations should receive the worst assignments and work schedules, and climb the same organizational ladder they climbed (even when the path has been blocked for decades by the Baby Boomers.) After all, this is what they did. The difference is that the younger employees believe that they are not likely to receive the same reciprocal benefits promised to older generations.

The Traditional generation also did not necessarily expect deep meaning from their jobs. Unlike the Boomers, who sought to change the world, many Traditionals merely like the familiarity of work, the routine, the camaraderie, and the coworkers. They like belonging to an organization and the status it brings.

Dr. Jon Warner and Anne Sandberg, authors of the *Generational Style Assessment (GSA)*[16], posit that this generation is now in the "winter" of their careers, and therefore their focus is on enlightenment and wisdom. They advise a "supporting" style of management for Traditional employees, which involves listening, offering support, and engaging in collaborative decision making.

Although the Traditional generation won't be in the workforce much longer (by 2011, many in this cohort will be retired), it is important to remember that members of this age group can still learn new skills. They do not want to be discounted or overlooked. Martin and Tulgan advise younger managers to be careful to respect their experience and wisdom. Remember that members of this generation may also possess vital expertise and procedural knowledge necessary to the smooth operation of the business. One might ask: does your organization have a plan in place to capture their knowledge or have them mentor younger workers before they retire? It might be time to formalize this knowledge transfer.

BABY BOOMERS: (born between 1946-64)

Once famous for saying, "Don't trust anyone over 30," boomers are now becoming the old guard in the workplace, the authority figures. Forever marked by the experience of the un-won war in Vietnam, Boomers entered the workplace under the traditional workplace set of rules, working under Traditional generation bosses until they paid their institutional dues. The workplace shifted under their feet, however, and they have had to adapt to a new set of workplace rules, mid-career.

Despite their well-earned reputation for rebellion, Martin and Tulgan point out that most boomers followed traditional work paths and sought employment with established organizations. Like the Traditional generation, they grew up in stable households, believing the world was "safe." Their bosses had standard operating procedures, and Boomers adapted to the status quo. Command-and-control leadership was the norm, and, Boomers had to toe the line and work hard. And did they ever work hard! Many became workaholics, leading very unbalanced lives, or foregoing family time (or even families), to succeed in the workforce.

Family-friendly work policies did not exist for them, so instead they reduced their family sizes (contributing to the gathering labor storm) and worked endless hours to compete against one another within their swollen demographic group. Young Boomers, seeing the unbalanced work emphasis of their older cohorts, began lobbying for more family-friendly workplaces and greater work/life balance. They still believed in job security and figured the system would take care of them through retirement, if they fulfilled their end of the bargain.

But then, just as they started to earn seniority and move into positions of authority, they were shell-shocked by the 1987 stock market crash and downsizing of the late 80s to early 90s. Hundreds of thousands of jobs disappeared, virtually overnight, and the promise of lifetime job security became a pipe dream. Many were forced by necessity to become job hoppers or to create their own businesses. Many Boomers had derived their sense of personal identity from their work and sacrificed life balance to achieve success, only to be blindsided by "disloyal" employers.

Coming of age in a work-world that valued seniority, and having paid their required dues, boomers find themselves in a changed work-world that now seems to reward speed and youth instead.

The Boomers want to know that management still honors their contributions. They are also, true to form, seeking opportunities for self-improvement and personal growth; employers who can provide these valued experiences will win their loyalty. Although the first Boomers will begin entering retirement soon, members of the Boomer generation will be in the workplace for another 5-20 years—perhaps even a bit longer if the demographic trends provide enough incentives for them to postpone retirement. While they remain in the workforce, they will want the same things we all want: ongoing challenges, the respect they've earned, and a sense of relevance.

Because this generation is in the "autumn" of their careers, Dr. Jon Warner and Anne Sandberg, recommend an "empowering" style of management. Workers of this age have generally "arrived," meaning they are often at the peak of their work lives, and they have attained a high level of expertise, confidence, and experience. This empowering style means allowing the employee to operate independently and simply to be available as needed.

GENERATION X (born between 1965-77)

There is no better example of the maxim that each generation reacts to the one preceding it than Generation X. Coming of age in the shadow of the Baby Boomers virtually ensured that this generation would be overlooked and ignored; like Prince Charles, they are the workplace "heirs apparent," waiting endlessly and impatiently to assume leadership.

The smallest generation since the Great Depression, Gen Xers are the products of the Baby Bust and the Birth Dearth. Upon graduation, they attempted to enter a work-world that was already saturated with the largest workforce generation in American history. They immediately grasped that their chances for upward mobility were blocked for the next thirty years by what has come to be called the "grey ceiling."

As Martin and Tulgan report, one Gen Xer complained,

> "'It's like we're all stuck in a silo. I've been working here for three years now, and any movement up that silo is blocked by you Boomers. You're going to be around for quite a while, so what am I supposed to do? I'm

ready to move now.' The Boomers sat in stunned silence at the audacity of this young woman; the few Xers in the audience surreptitiously nodded their heads in agreement."[17]

Careerwise, however, after graduating from college with degrees as credible as their predecessors, Gen Xers faced a work-world that didn't need them. Many were shunted into low-skilled, low-paying positions (so-called "McJobs") for which they were eminently overqualified. They quickly ascertained that the traditional career path had little to offer them.

On top of the bad demographic odds, they were trying to begin their careers just as the major downsizing events thrust more experienced Boomers out on the streets. As a result, they had little trust in the implied employer-employee lifetime contract. They responded by becoming a generation of "free agents" and entrepreneurs, striking out on their own.

Their childhoods were much different than those of Traditionals and Boomers. According to Martin and Tulgan, Generation X was the most unsupervised generation in American history—the original "latchkey kids." They were expected to look after themselves before and after school while their parents chased fulfillment and climbed the corporate ladder.

Xers were "born during one of the most blatantly anti-child phases in U.S. history." Their traditional and Older Boomer parents had "the highest divorce and abortion rates, highest number of dual-income families, and most permissive parenting habits in our history."[18] In response, Xers developed the view that the world was "unsafe."

As a result, they grew up to be self-reliant, fending for themselves. This necessary "fend-for-myself" attitude turned out to be remarkably valuable within the changing work-world. Xers have always been accustomed to taking care of themselves, which ironically turned out to be excellent training for the independent career paths they would pursue within the challenging work environment they faced.

Perhaps the most defining characteristic of this generation's "coming-of-age" years is the *lack* of a defining moment, although younger Gen Xers may point to the tearing down of the Berlin Wall as a crucial moment in expanding their view of possibilities.

Although Gen Xers were initially viewed by older generations as disloyal slackers who were unwilling to "toe the line" or "pay their dues," they have emerged as the most innovative generation of our lifetime, ushering in a new wave of American entrepreneurialism. Their hallmark is flexibility; they are also independent, skilled with technology, and adaptable. (Not coincidentally, these adjectives could also be used to describe the modern workplace.)

Luckily, their coming-of-age coincided with the birth of the internet, which facilitated their "free agent" career trajectories. They eagerly embraced this liberating new technology, emerging as wonder-kid, "dot.com" entrepreneurs during the 1990s.

It's true, as the stereotype suggests that Xers are prone to switching jobs: nearly 18 million change jobs annually and their average tenure on a job is just three years.[19] Other studies indicate young workers will change jobs eight to fourteen times before they reach the age of 32. Xers are very unlikely to stay with organizations that fail to tap into their creativity and entrepreneurial urges; they like to keep their options open, which make it a challenge for employers to retain them.

Unlike Traditionals, they lack strong attachments to institutions. Remember: these are the children of many Boomer parents who were laid off, downsized, right-sized and outsourced mid-career after years of loyal service. These Xers learned early on that their best security came from relying on their own resourcefulness.

Gen Xers demand work/life balance from their employers. Unlike Boomers and Traditionals, they are not obsessed with climbing the corporate ladder, since they tend to have a cynical mistrust of institutions anyway. They want to achieve success on their own terms and part of what they consider "being successful" is having a successful "lifestyle."

This means having freedom, including time for family, friends, travel and hobbies. They are not content to sacrifice their personal or family lives for their employers, since that neglect is what characterized their own childhoods. Unlike Traditionals, who value "face time," they prefer to be paid for the results they achieve rather than for the hours they put in; they may work well independently and virtually, in remote locations, or in telecommuting arrangements.

The free agency mindset that Xers adopted in response to the difficult economic climate they encountered at the start of their careers didn't disappear as the economy and their career fortunes improved; instead, it went mainstream. A "hidden" freelance job market emerged, thanks largely to the internet, and a new generation learned how to make a living at home, wearing pajamas, sipping chai teas, lattes and cappuccinos.

Generation X employees bring continual learning skills which is necessary to keep pace with rapid technological change. They are frequently innovators in the workplace, as well as risk-takers; this places them at odds with the Traditional generation. Even within established organizations, they bring an entrepreneurial flair for starting new ventures. All of these characteristics, coupled with their relative youth (making them young enough to help ride out the Perfect Labor Storm) make them extremely valuable employees to recruit and retain.

Xers are results-oriented and lean-focused, continually looking for new ways to achieve goals rather than following established and pointless procedures. They are likely to agree with the phrase that it is possible to "work smarter, not harder." In other words, they want to work on things that add or create value, not just doing things to keep busy.

Xers have proven that they can achieve results and "get the job done;" now they're ready to move into leadership positions. For too long, Xers have been the overlooked "new kid" on the block, or the "wunderkind." At this point in their careers, they seek increasing spheres of responsibility and are ready to move onto center stage. These younger generational cohorts are going to require increased responsibility; otherwise, managers risk losing them to the competition.

Other ways to motivate and retain Gen Xers include offering nontraditional work arrangements that facilitate work/life balance. If organizations can offer flexible work arrangements—including schedules, assignments, locations, coworkers—they can hook Xers into a long-term employment relationship.

Customization is the watchword of the modern workplace and it will increasingly apply to career paths. By offering customized organizational charts, rather than the cookie-cutter hierarchies of the past, businesses can provide enough different, satisfying alternatives to retain this talented generation of employees.

Xers seek responsibility, challenge, growth, and mobility. Mobility doesn't always have to be upward, however. Not everyone wants to move into management, especially if the "advancement" comes with increased time commitments. Organizations that can redefine traditional career paths to accommodate new lifestyle patterns will have the best chance to attract and hold on to key talent among younger cohorts.

Martin and Tulgan suggest that Gen Xers may be open to lateral moves that fulfill key values, such as ongoing learning. What other options are at a companies' disposal to recognize, reward and develop young people who won't wait another five to ten years to move through the "silo" of the organization? Offering high producing Xers opportunities to advance their careers in ways that make sense to them is a key retention strategy.

Another key to managing intergenerational conflict is to provide mentoring relationships and a "coaching" managerial style. For one thing, Xers want access to decision makers. The traditional top-down hierarchical managerial style is not effective with younger generations in the workplace.

Consultants agree that Xers place a high value on opportunities to build lasting relationships with wise and experienced mentors; this is a great way to bring the different generations into positive and productive collaboration while increasing the transfer of organizational knowledge to the heirs apparent.

Dr. Jon Warner and Anne Sandberg advise using a "steering" style of management for this age group, which is in the "summer" of their careers. This age group is frequently struggling with direction and benefits from being given broad frameworks, within which they can accomplish goals on their own.

GENERATION Y or the MILLENNIAL/NET GENERATION (born between 1978-1990)

The youngest workers, members of Generation Y, are on the scene and demanding respect. They have many of the same characteristics of Generation X, only even more so. Described as being "high maintenance," (some might say, "spoiled") they're quite vocal and willing to share their opinions about everything. And they expect management to care. And to respond. Quickly, please.

Why shouldn't they expect this? They are used to the instant gratification of the technological resources that have always been at their disposal. While answering machines changed communication habits for the Traditionals, beepers, voice mail and fax machines revolutionized the modes of staying in touch for Boomers. Then came the mobile "bag" phone in the 80s and cell phone in the 90s. Today we have a generation that has grown up with "instant" messaging, staying in constant contact with others anywhere in the world through PDAs (personal digital assistants) and smartphones—virtual entertainment centers that combine communication, music, and video in the palm of your hand. They are accustomed to sharing their opinions, favorite music and live video with the world and making their voices heard instantly, about even the most mundane topics. Through self-created blogs, websites, and MySpace accounts, they are connected to the entire world, anytime. The world is literally at their fingertips. In contrast with the "Era of Limits" that defined the so-called "Geezers" (according to authors Bennis and Thomas) these "Geeks" grew up during the "Era of Options."

They can easily gain instant access to people and information around the world, providing them with a sense of empowerment, and speed, that may overwhelm less techno-savvy older generations. They really are the "net" generation, with a global outlook, although the events of September 11, 2001 certainly left an indelible imprint on their collective psyches.

Gen Y, like older generations, experienced the sort of close parenting that eluded Generation X. Thanks to more family-friendly workplace policies, and a natural reaction against unsupervised children, Generation Y enjoyed closer parental involvement, bordering on over-indulgent. The terms "helicopter" parent and "snowplow" parent have been coined to describe their parents who have continually hovered overhead and cleared the way for this young generation. Reports abound of parents going with their children on job interviews, serving as agents to negotiate compensation packages, and constantly IM-ing (Instant Messaging) their kids in class. The combination of technological access with parental backing has created a phenomenal sense of empowerment.

Influenced by education-minded Boomer parents, Gen Yers believe that education is the key to their success, and they're poised to be lifelong learners. Generation Y is *even more* entrepreneurial and techno-savvy than Gen X. They also love challenging work and creative expression and they, too, value freedom and flexibility. Martin and Tulgan assert, "They hate micromanagement. And they are poised to be the most demanding generation in history."[20]

This "Digital Generation" is ready to learn anywhere, anytime, and is even more comfortable with technology than Generation X. While the Gen Xer never grew up in a world without ATMs and personal computers, Gen Ys have always had the Internet.

A distinctive characteristic of Generation Y is that they demand immediate feedback, and they expect to gain a sense of accomplishment hourly. They thrive on challenging work and creative expression. They're more than willing to tell management how to improve their workplace policies and procedures, which can rub experienced, older employees the wrong way. Savvy managers need to provide them with appropriate outlets to share their insights because they also possess the ability to be great team players.

What this all means is that Generation Y is used to getting attention, and they are demanding it in the workplace. They want to have a close, highly-responsive relationship with their superiors, like they had with their parents, and the personal relationship with their boss is very important to them. They don't respond well to the traditional Command and Control management style. Martin and Tulgan point out, "They consistently tell us they have difficulty with older managers who condescendingly correct them or even yell and scream."[21]

They want managers to spend time getting to know them and their capabilities, and to develop a personal mentoring relationship with them. In keeping with the atomization of the internet, they want their jobs to be even more personalized, and even more customized than their predecessors, Generation X.

Consistent with the age-old generation gap, this younger generation predictably sees the older generation as resisting change and being stuck in procedures. (So some things never really change; at least we can count on that). They are always seeking shortcuts and striving to get more done faster. (They may seem to older employees to be stuck on "fast forward").

Managers are advised to consistently provide constructive feedback to this cohort—the more immediate, the better. Accustomed to email, instant messaging, and text messages, Gen Y expects to stay in constant contact with others, including management. Executive secretaries and middle management, the traditional organizational gatekeepers for senior management, must now function as portals of access. This may mean adaptation for older managers accustomed to being "out of touch" after hours or on weekends and preserving their time for board room meetings and golf outings. Today's VIP list must include the up-and-coming workforce.

As is always the case with new employees or younger generations, the older generation may find themselves having to explain the rationale behind certain policies or being challenged to justify every procedure and explain why things are the way they are. It will be most productive if managers see this as an opportunity to question the status quo and a chance to consider innovation, rather than as an impertinent imposition.

Millennials not only value but demand opportunities for ongoing training and development. Like Generation X, these Millennials see "job security" as meaning constantly updating their skills to remain marketable. They are always looking for better opportunities, elsewhere. Finally, whereas older employees understandably want rewards to be tied to seniority, younger employees want to be rewarded for their performance and results.

Dr. Jon Warner and Anne Sandberg, authors of the *Generational Style Assessment*, propose that members of Generation Y are in the "spring" of their careers, and, as such, are filled with enthusiasm and interested in discovery and exploration. They recommend using what they call a highly interactive "building" managerial style, in which communication is clear and focused, as well as energetic and engaging. Additionally there should be a lot of give and take in communicating.

Cam Marston, a multigenerational communications and marketing consultant, points out that many younger workers have had an extended adolescence—as much as a decade longer than their predecessors. They marry later and stay in school longer, and as a result, feel less pressure to select a career in their twenties. Whereas earlier generations were told to "get a job" and become "self-sufficient," today's young workers are being encouraged to find a job that makes them happy or that offers "self-fulfillment." Marston's interesting view is that Boomers sought self-sufficiency first, and hoped to stumble upon self-fulfillment, while the Millenial's view is reversed: seek self-fulfillment first, and hope to become self-sufficient eventually. To complicate matters, more and more Millennial employees are finding self-fulfillment outside of work.[22]

Some other interesting differences include perspectives on time. Boomers were apt to define a hard worker by counting the number of hours devoted to work. A 60-hour work week meant you were on track for a highly valued promotion. Younger workers measure work ethic by whether they complete required jobs on time, and they are likely to perceive office gatherings as interfering with their personal time, rather than as a reward. Promotions mean little to them. Gen Xers are particularly cynical about meetings and view them mainly as a waste of time and "posturing sessions full of hooey."[23] Boomers and Traditionals still value them. Boomers think work is serious; younger workers expect it to be "fun." Boomers dislike teams (not to be confused with work groups); younger workers enjoy them.[24] Boomers define themselves by their work and work to pay the bills. Gen Xers also work to pay the bills, but they assume the job they have will not last forever.[25] Thus, they work to learn new skills that will help them obtain their next job. They are loyal to people, not jobs. According to Marston, "When a Gen Xer finds a mentor, loyalty will follow."[26] Generation Y is not working to pay the bills, but to afford a lifestyle. Work to them is a means to an end, not an end in itself. With all this in mind, organizations will need to possess adaptable and flexible leaders to be able to motivate and manage such disparate workers.

Managing the Future Workforce

There is no doubt about it: management styles are going to have to adapt to handle not only the coming changes in demographics, but also the changes in the composition of the future workforce. One cannot successfully manage everyone the same way; adjustments must be made. Younger workers will have to be managed differently than employees were managed in the past. This is an emerging field of interest, and different experts have different views on the subject; time will tell what is the best approach. What follows are examples of a few generational styles and responses for managers to consider:

Warner and Sandberg advocate using four distinctly different styles for effectively managing the different generations currently occupying the workforce.[27] These styles are dependent not only upon the cohort differences that characterize each current generation, but also upon general issues of lifespan human development. Younger workers are always going to have different issues, interests, and concerns than older workers, due to their own particular challenges.

These four styles, which Warner and Sandberg label "Supporting", "Empowering", "Steering", and "Building," correspond respectively with the Traditional Generation, the Baby Boomer Generation, Generation X and the Millennials (or Generation Y.) These styles are based on a quadrant model which contrasts the levels of *focus, clarity, energy,* and *engagement* employed. Let's look briefly at each style, and the corresponding age of life for which it is most effective.

The **Supporting** Style is most appropriate to use with people who are in their fifties or beyond. Warner and Sandberg describe these as the "Reflective" Years, during which older workers are generally more relaxed and less competitive. Having already passed through a midlife reevaluation, many of these workers are using their wisdom and experience to reprioritize their lives, redefine their dreams, and make a significant impact. Still capable of contributing, the Supporting Style of management is best because it affirms their role by offering strong support and encouragement for these individuals to share their expertise and wisdom with others. The Supporting style is high in energy and engagement, which is best directed towards encouraging the older employee to contribute accumulated wisdom and expertise, rather than on clarifying specific performance goals or targets. The Supportive style emphasizes listening and engaging in collaborative decision-making, recognizing that the older team member is likely to dominate and control the communication.

The **Empowering** Style is recommended for workers in their 40s and above; this would include most of the Baby Boomers in the current workforce. This management style is low in both focus and clarity *and* in energy and engagement, in recognition of the fact that employees in this age bracket are in the peak of their working years. Generally speaking, midlife employees need less support at work; their years of experience make them large contributors who need little supervision. Workers in this age group are said to be in the "Autumn" of their careers, which means that this time period is characterized by anxiety and reevaluation. This corresponds with a need for more freedom which is just what the Empowering Style provides. The Empowering Manager will allow "Autumn" workers to take charge of their own lives and careers, as much as possible.

During the "Summer" years of employment, employees respond best to a **Steering** Style of management. This is because these employees (who would currently be Generation X, mainly in their 30s) are in their productive, growth years. Warner and Sandberg describe these years as being marked by intense and significant personal and work life progression and growth. Because these are extremely busy years, with many family responsibilities, work-life issues are likely to be particularly important to this age group. These are the career building, ladder climbing years, during which "getting ahead" is very important to many workers. Therefore, the Steering Style of management offers workers in this age group what they need: high focus and clarity which involves steering the employee towards the most important goals and objectives, coupled with a relatively low-intensity, laid back communication style. Because these workers have already acquired considerable experience and expertise, they do not require the same level of "handling" that the youngest group of workers will require. For the most part, if given clear and broad frameworks or guidelines, these workers can be left to accomplish goals on their own.

Finally, the youngest workers in an organization require what is termed a **Building** Style of management and supervision. This is because these employees (mainly in their 20s) are in what Warner and Sandberg call the "Spring" or "dream years" of their careers, which typically includes a period of exploration. Workers in this age group are likely to be energetic and enthusiastic, optimistic and open-minded. Unfortunately, they can also be reckless and selfish. Because workers in this demographic are setting a life direction, forming their life dreams and have acquired little work experience, they respond well to a highly involved managerial style. Definitely high maintenance, this group of workers requires high levels of all four management inputs: clarity, focus, energy and engagement. Work expectations should be made crystal clear with follow-up and ongoing communication. These workers prefer to have a highly communicative relationship with their superiors, characterized by give-and-take.

Anne Sandberg offers some additional guidelines for how to handle typical intergenerational career conflicts that may occur between older managers and younger employees. Let's consider some of the most common traits of younger workers and look at some of the best ways of handling these in the workforce.

Characteristic	How to manage it
Expect lots of praise	Use praise and recognition as a motivator and they will work harder
Likely to be frank, lacking in tact or subtlety	Be frank with them and consider their suggestions
Informal dress and manners	Explain clearly what is appropriate (or inappropriate)—when and why
Want a fun work environment	Consider their suggestions
Work-life balance	Provide flexible work arrangements and other creative solutions
"Follow your dreams" attitude	Provide mentoring and help them set realistic goals
Not motivated by sense of "duty"	Phrase requirements as opportunity for personal growth and the acquisition of new knowledge and skills
Technology oriented	Give them technological tools and challenges[28]

Cam Marston offers further targeted advice to address this issue in his book, *Motivating the "What's In It For Me" Workforce: Manage Across the Generational Divide and Increase Profits*. Crucial to managing younger workers effectively, says Marston, is recognizing their different loyalty and priority systems:

"Like Gen Xers, New Millennials have changed the definition of loyalty yet again. Their loyalty is often to the person for whom they work, because that person is leading them to their goals and is helping them construct the road map that will get them where they want to go. Past generations have had to create this path on their own. But New Millennials relied on their parents to do it, and now in the workplace, they're relying on their bosses, their substitute parents, to help them. Like Gen Xers, they're loyal to people, not to companies. *When New Millennials decide to leave, they don't quit the company; they quit the boss. If the boss isn't helping them get where they want to go, they're off."*[29]

This "quit the boss, not the company" philosophy change caught the attention of senior management in 1999 when Marcus Buckingham and Curt Coffman exposed the fallacies of standard management thinking in *First, Break All the Rules: What the World's Greatest Managers Do Differently.* The authors culled their observations from more than 80,000 interviews conducted by Gallup during the previous 25 years. In this landmark change in management thinking, Buckingham and Coffman determined that **front-line** managers—not the company itself—are the key to attracting and retaining talented employees.

Marston warns that managers of younger employees can expect to be tested routinely, because Generations X and Y want to find out if authority figures are genuine and worthy of trust. (Remember that they have grown up with such disillusionments as Watergate, a presidential impeachment over lying, Enron and WorldCom, and most recently the war in Iraq.) This has made them suspicious of hierarchy and authority. Once an authority figure has been proven trustworthy to younger generations, however, they can be quite loyal.

Be prepared for different valuations on time in the workplace. Older employees are more likely to think they are doing a good job if they put in many face hours at work, regardless of their levels of productivity. Younger workers are going to expect to be able to leave if they accomplish the tasks they were expected to complete. "Battle lines between the generations are sometimes drawn over how much time it should actually take to *accomplish* the job. Generation X and New Millennials believe that the less time spent to get the job done right, the better. The Gen Xers and New Millennials view long hours as inefficient and unnecessary if the job can be completed during normal business hours. The younger employees want to know, "Are you paying me to be here or are you paying me to get the job done? Why does it matter where and how long I work as long as I get the job done?" It really is a question of effectiveness. "Generation X and New Millennials will almost always cite productivity, not time spent working, as a standard of measurement for the work done."[30] This can be challenging for Boomer bosses, who often will offer rewards based on other factors.

Marston advises that, "if they can do the job at odd hours and get it done to the satisfaction of their superiors, super. They shouldn't be restricted to the typical 8-to-5 workday. Likewise, if they can finish their job early to the satisfaction of their superiors, the remainder of the day should be theirs."[31] Will your organization be receptive to this scenario? The answer matters, because to the younger generations, time is as valuable a commodity as money.

To be a successful manager and boss in the twenty-first century, one will have to learn to play by some new rules. Consider implementing the following suggestions, which are based upon Cam Marston's years of multigenerational consultation:

- Use Clear and Straightforward Language

  o Instructions presented as "suggestions" will be perceived as "suggestions" by younger employees. If you mean, "Do it," you need to say so. Spell out exactly what you expect. Then be flexible about *how* they do it.

- Celebrate Achievements

  o Find a way to measure and reward outstanding productivity

- Forge personal relationships with younger employees

  o Thinking of yourself as a "coach," helping your employee reach mutually favorable goals, may be the best way to go.

- Emphasize learning opportunities
- Harness the power of technology in the workplace
- Ask employees for their input and consider their ideas seriously
- Younger employees may be "thin-skinned" and may need to be reprimanded differently—preferably privately, and in a supportive fashion

According to Cam Marston, if companies can keep employees on the job for four years, their turnover numbers will drop dramatically, so this should be a key goal for your organizations.[32] One of the best ways to do this is by spending time getting to know your employees. Do you know what their real goals and aspirations are? Do you know about their families and outside-work lives? These factors can be crucial in the make-or-break decisions to stay with a current position or seek greener pastures elsewhere. An open-door policy for the airing of grievances or bouncing off ideas is also highly appreciated by younger generations. Even better, be proactive and seek out your employees, rather than waiting for them to come to you. Topics of discussion should also include more than just work, since lifestyle and work-life balance issues are so important to younger workers.

When faced with special requests from younger employees, Marston advises not caving in, but negotiating: "The answer isn't 'Yes'; it's 'Yes', but what are you going to do for me?' The first time you bargain with an employee, you might think that person will quit. But in fact, she or he is impressed with the negotiation. The difference is that when you grant everything asked for, you're seen as a pushover—and pushovers rarely get any true respect. If, however, you were to blankly say 'No,' you'd be seen as inflexible—and no one wants to work with an inflexible person. Negotiation is the way to go, and your people will respect you for it."[33]

The organization and the leader who is able to adapt to the needs and expectations of the future workforce will gain a competitive foothold within the labor marketplace. That's assuming, however, that companies can attract the younger employees in the first place.

SPECIAL OFFER FOR READERS OF THIS BOOK:
As a special "Thank You" for reading *The Perfect Labor Storm 2.0*,
Success Performance Solutions is pleased to offer a complimentary sample of
the "Generational Style Assessment." To request your FREE GSA, visit:
www.super-solutions.com/freegenerationalstyleassessment.asp

Attracting Young Employees in a Seller's Job Market

To survive in the coming labor storm, one's business is going to have to shift not only their message, but also how their message is delivered, to have the best chance of attracting the next generation of employees.

First off, you are going to have to assess your current situation. What are your specific hiring challenges? What is the coming retirement scenario in your organization? Are there specific positions within your company that are always hard to fill or keep filled?

Getting the attention of the younger generation can be difficult. Unlike their predecessors, they are a complex group with diverse interests. They already receive multiple messages, often simultaneously, through a variety of outlets. Their priorities are also entirely different from those of older generations.

Happily, recent research by the Ad Council provides some insight into the characteristics that define today's young workers, which can make it easier to reach out and connect with them. Understanding the next generation is going to be crucial to your organization's attempts to garner their commitment.

The key to reaching young potential workers is to tap into their interests and to speak to their concerns. The Ad Council suggests rethinking your expectations, because Gen-X and New Millennial workers have different views of success. Their highest values include individuality, personal freedom, flexibility, and ownership of their free time.

It is important to be very clear about your organizational mission and vision, because younger generations are looking for a cause to feel passionate about. Once you have crafted a compelling message, you will need to communicate this in multiple ways to reach the highly fragmented young adult market. The traditional avenues of advertising probably won't cut it. You'll need to reach young adults in the ways they prefer to communicate, including social networks like Facebook, internet chat rooms, listservs, bulletin boards, and email.[34]

The Ad Council's research points out that younger workers are more diverse than the general population. Both Generation X and Generation Y are generally considered to be fiercely independent, preferring to trust in themselves. Generation X is realistic, even pessimistic (having graduated right into a recession). Generation Y is similar, but more optimistic, with more social involvement and high empowerment. These younger cohorts are not followers or conformists. Both cohorts have strong individualistic streaks."[35]

These young adults are under high amounts of stress, and they live a fast-paced and hectic lifestyle. They are accustomed to being inundated by information and are constantly "tethered" to mobile phones, PDAs, and mp3 players, which may leave them with the feeling that they can never escape. The combined effect creates a craving for work/life balance at younger ages. You are likely to find that there is no single, unifying cause around which today's young people rally, as was true of prior generations. Instead, you will have to seek out your target employees with specially-tailored, niche-driven messages.

Remember as well that younger employees are likely to expect that a portion of their social life will occur at work, so they will be evaluating your corporate culture as much as the pay or options for promotion. What kind of social environment can your organization offer them?

You will need to evaluate your organization realistically on the following factors which are considered very important by the younger generation of employees: flexible scheduling; flat hierarchical structures with access to decision makers; rewards and recognition; and openness to input. In your workplace, is the process as important as the product? Is it fun to work at your organization? These are the factors that are going to matter to the employees you need to be able to attract.

Part of your strategy is going to have to involve developing messages that resonate strongly with young adults. A personal approach is best, and then you are going to have to establish a plan to ensure that your target audience hears your message, including using local media, direct mail, the Internet, and even unconventional marketing approaches like My Space, Facebook, and Second Life, to reach young adults.[36]

To attract the attention of young workers, you will need to communicate clearly your organization's passion. Young people are impressed by an organization that knows its reason for being; by stating explicitly what you stand for, you show them your belief in your mission. Passion is extremely powerful in attracting young people—especially this generation. The Ad Council suggests including young people as advisors in the communication and outreach planning process. This may be one of the most effective techniques you can implement, and you're apt to be impressed by young people's energy, optimism, and creativity.[37]

Marketing Your Organization

To market your organization effectively, you will want to position it in the same way in which a product is "positioned." This is how you make any "product" stand out in a crowded marketplace. During the coming Perfect Labor Storm, the marketplace of hiring organizations is likely to become very crowded indeed.

Proper positioning provides a clear sense of how your product—in this case, your organization—is different from, and presumably better than, the competition. Once you are clear about how to position your organization, make sure that you consistently incorporate this message in all of your advertising and communications efforts. Ideally, you want your target employee to hear a consistent message about your organization from many angles.

Ad Council research suggests a number of possible platforms that should resonate with young people:

- Try to position your organization as people who have a common passion, rather than as an institution. Young adults are much more likely to gravitate toward small organizations and people they can connect with than to large and (in their mind) nameless, faceless organizations.
- Emphasize certain individual employees and the contributions they've made, and position your organization around them. An effective campaign might involve asking, "Who is (your company)?" and then answering that question in a series of different images or vignettes. This type of positioning can be quite effective, especially if you need to correct false impressions.
- You could also position your organization as being all about ideas, since today's young adults respond strongly to the power of ideas. They have learned that having the right idea can make someone very successful.

It's also worthwhile to test potential positioning by discussing ideas with a group of young people you might be trying to attract to your organization.[38]

Young adults respond favorably to humor, music, meaningful content, and positive, actionable messages, according to the Ad Council's research. They are also looking for messages that show cause and effect or people accomplishing goals.[39] Other advice includes maintaining authenticity (don't try to be something you're not or try to be all things to all people) and using real people in communication, since young people tend to be quite receptive to their messages. Further strategies suggested by the Ad Council:

- **Let them decide.** The most effective ads today tend to make young people feel as if they have made a decision. This is very empowering.
- **Stay focused.** The message is lost if it is too broad or confusing. Given all of the stimuli in their lives, young people typically have no patience for anything but laser-sharp focus. Your message should be as clear and specific as possible.
- **Be true to yourself.** Be true to your organizational brand and your values.
- **Make it easy for young people to learn more about your organization.** Be sure to provide a local phone number or address, a toll-free number, or a Web site.

- **Don't try to mimic young people's language**, unless the person delivering the message is also from that age group. Young people see right through adults who try to use slang in hopes of appealing to them.
- **Don't over-promise**. They would much prefer that you "tell it like it is."

Many youth marketers have found that a combination of facts and emotions work best when talking to young people.[40]

Delivering your message

Reaching young potential employees is not easy, but if you follow these guidelines, you will improve your chances of success. If you're near a college town, your organization should consider offering internship opportunities to students. It's also worthwhile to contact local college marketing companies; they may be able, and willing, to share insights into the college populations in your area.

Be alert for influential young people within your organization. Keep an eye out for those young men and women who seem to exude charisma or to be "opinion leaders" among their age group. When you identify them, see if they are willing to help by serving as spokespeople for your organization. Of course, you will want to equip your chosen spokespeople with appropriate and well-thought-out position papers or talking points about your organization and issues. It is imperative to keep your spokespeople up-to-date on important developments, and to offer expert training in public speaking or media relations. And be sure to show your appreciation to them![41]

Reaching Your Audience

Reaching the younger adult audience is more difficult than reaching older generations, because they do not use the traditional media in the same way. According to the Ad Council, "The bottom line is that it's getting harder and harder to break through to young people today. They are enthusiastic consumers of the media, but they've got a mind-boggling array of choices to make every time they visit a newsstand, flip on the TV, or boot up their computers."[42]

As you will read shortly, marketing jobs to young workers requires a multi-media, multi-faceted approach, customized and targeted depending on the jobs, geography, and even socio-economic level. Hiring managers will want to pay attention to the relative costs associated with each recruiting strategy. Searching for the right candidates in the wrong medium can add unnecessary spending to the already skyrocketing cost to recruit, hire and retain workers.

One example of the diligence hiring managers must undertake before choosing an advertising medium points to a major discrepancy between two studies. While the Ad Council suggests that radio and magazines are the two most effective mediums for reaching young people, Staffing.org in its *2007 Recruiting Metrics and Performance Benchmark Report* states that job boards and personal referrals (which include employee referrals), according to nearly 80% of job seekers, are the best sources to fill job openings. In the report, career fairs and broadcast media were the *least effective*. In fact, less than 5% of job seekers listed "other media and career fairs" as the best venue for recruitment. The best recruitment solution then will be a matrix of media, customized for your company, geography, and industry through a series of trial-and-error mini-campaigns.

Radio

"Radio remains one of the best, most targeted ways to reach young adults," according to the Ad Council. "Marketers of all sorts take advantage of this relatively low-cost way to deliver their messages, and young adults listen an average of almost 23 hours per week. Plus, young people are more likely to identify with their radio stations than with other media outlets."[43]

It is worthwhile noting that while some young adults listen to traditional radio, many more are wired to Internet and satellite stations or get their information primarily from podcasts. Before investing in radio ads, print media, or online job boards, you might want to consider your target audience. What are the jobs you are hoping to fill? How techno-savvy are your candidates? What demographic and socio-economic group do they belong to? This information will help you to decide if radio advertising makes sense for your organization.

The Internet

The current generation of young workers is wired. They appreciate anything that is instantly at their fingertips. These young people are online more than any other age demographic, so your organization had better remember this crucial fact when seeking to reach them. According to recent census data, 32% of 18-24 year olds currently use the Internet—that's almost 8 million users—compared to only 22% of the adult population. And young people trust the Web more than newspapers or TV, according to Project Vote Smart. The Web—specifically e-mail—tends to be one of the best ways to communicate with young people over time. Unlike physical addresses, Web addresses are portable and young people tend to keep the same e-mail addresses even as they move around. Also, young people have become accustomed to checking their email boxes on a regular basis, so your message is likely to get to them relatively quickly."[44]

An innovative way to reach young college age, and new college grads is to offer online meetings and group discussions. Developing an online seminar through a large campus organization ensures that, at the very least, most of that organization will be in attendance. Offering something new and different to students will not only put you ahead of the pack, but will make your business highly desirable. Consider hosting an online collegiate job fair, where businesses from all over the area (and other parts of the state/nation) are represented. Resumes could easily be exchanged via file transfers, and no one feels awkwardly out of place in their suits and ties (or flip flops and shorts). This also eliminates the worry of face-to-face confrontation. Prospective employees and employers will probably feel more comfortable chatting online in their own homes and rooms, plus this can also give each employer the opportunity to talk to several people at one time, or only one at a time.

Another big trend among the current generation is Facebook, Myspace, and Second Life. Facebook (as described from the website www.facebook.com) "is a social utility that connects you with the people around you. Facebook is made up of many networks, each based around a *workplace, region, high school* or *college*." The premise of Facebook is simple: a user creates a profile with information about themselves, then the user can easily find other people they know and "friend" them. It's like a virtual rolodex full of everything your hardcopy can't contain: all important numbers, dates, and information; also pictures, comments, and interest groups. Myspace (*www.myspace.com*) is very similar to Facebook, but MySpace grants more freedom to the design of the webpage (i.e. basic html and flash programming).

Second Life is different from the other two online communities, because Second Life is its own virtual world. Every day new entrants are joining the second life 'metaverse' and starting businesses. In Second Life almost anything is possible, which is why many businesses are setting up 'shop' and holding meetings with clients from all over the world, selling products and authorizing transactions.

And just when you thought you might have heard it all, the first virtual job fair of its kind was held in Second Life during the month of May 2007. Candidates from all over the world, represented by avatars (an Internet user's virtual self), participated by meeting "avatar" recruiters from Sodhexo, eBay, HP, Microsoft, T-Mobile, and Verizon. (To read more about "What is Second Life," go to *www.super-solutions. com/whatissecondlife.asp.*)

Utilizing these new media is vital to getting the attention of today's younger generation. Corporations such as Apple and Dell run promotions on Facebook, and many musical artists and even business leaders maintain a MySpace presence to offer a 'blog' of events which not only makes them seem more down-to-earth but also more easily accessible.

Incidentally, avoid relying on phone calls as the predominant means of communication with prospects and instead use e-mail to stay in contact. College students are constantly on cell phones, but cell phones also cost valuable minutes during day time hours. This can result in a tendency to avoid making phone calls to LAN and other service provider lines, especially at the end of the month. Alternatively, most universities have e-mail kiosks virtually everywhere and/or free wireless internet access.

Magazines

Magazines are an effective vehicle for reaching young people, although this market is fairly fragmented. Magazine messages can be niche marketed and last longer than cyber-advertising. You also have more space in which to state your message effectively.

Local Media

Of course, there are the traditional television and radio outlets, but consider tapping into college media. College radio stations are much more targeted than the local media, and advertising on them is also much cheaper. Naturally, you will want to take advantage of annual college job fairs. These are excellent opportunities to showcase your organization; just make sure that you present the right image!

Traditional Newspapers

This is probably your worst bet to attract young workers, since traditional newspaper readership is low among this demographic. It still might be a good medium to attract older Boomers and Traditionals, as well as low-tech, low wage employees where the technology skills of the talent pool might be limited. For young workers, college or alternative newspapers are well read. Try advertising in the online versions of newspapers, which are generally more appealing to young readers.

Direct Mail

Direct mail offers you a targeted means of reaching your consumer, but remember that the young adult market is a highly mobile and transient group. Because they move around more than average, you have to make sure that you have current, accurate addresses to reach them.

Unconventional Methods

Think about where young adults go in your community and take your message to them. This might include posting your flyers on college kiosks, in campus bookstores, in hair salons, art galleries or coffee shops. Then, try some even more unexpected places. The Ad Council suggests posting flyers at local events such as "parties and shows, or recreational areas such as skate parks and basketball courts. You can consider graffiti, or chalk drawings on high-trafficked sidewalks. You may even leverage a partnership arrangement to get your message printed on CDs or video games, both of which are popular with young people."[45]

First Impressions Are Important

Regardless of how successful your recruitment campaign is, companies must be ready to respond. As common-sensical as that sounds, Staffing.org reported in April 2007 that "communications and follow-up continue to be abysmal and undermine candidate regard and interest in employers. Just shy of 500,000 job seekers gave employers a rating of 1 (out of 5) on communications and follow-up and less than a 3 (out of 5) on scheduling interviews and accuracy and completeness of job descriptions. All too common were no responses, not meeting commitments, and treating candidates like "tele-marketing representatives" until candidates were requested to schedule an interview or until a job offer was made.

Reaching and engaging the next generation of employees is going to become an essential skill to help your organization survive the coming Perfect Labor Storm. Understanding who your audience is, and where they spend their time, will be critical information in recruiting new and replacement workers. With the right message, carefully crafted to your audience and delivered through effective media outlets, you will increase your chances of finding the right people for your organization.

Advice From a "New Millennial"

Any good marketer knows that the best way to find out what your target market likes and expects is to *ask them*. With this in mind, I asked our summer intern, a third year college student at the University of Pittsburgh, to provide the following "Five Strategies for Success" for recruiting young workers. You might be surprised not only by what you learn about the point of view of an in-demand young employee, but also by what your competition is up to.

Refining Recruitment for Young Adults: Five Strategies for Success

Young adults these days are not just worried about getting a degree-related job post graduation; they are increasingly concerned with field-related summer and semester internships. Since many of these young adults are students currently enrolled at universities and colleges around the nation, they are eager to gain valuable experience and apply their newly-acquired skill set to the "real world."

For businesses, taking on summer interns can result in a fairly cheap, educated, part-time labor force. And for young adults, taking a summer internship will yield substantial business knowledge, the application of school work, and most importantly, resume development. It's a win-win situation. When you find a good intern, be clear and specific about job expectations. Keep in mind that although they are educated, many students really have no idea "what you do;" keep clear goals and instructions in mind and then let 'em go. So what types of ways are successful businesses attracting these potential employees?

1. **Businesses are going directly to the source**. A good way to connect with students is by going directly to the universities and colleges. Many schools have several job fairs, which offer the opportunity for students to get associated with businesses in their field. With little to no work (other than a poster display, etc.), businesses can obtain several resumes of potential candidates. It's as easy as that. Getting involved with these job fairs isn't too difficult either. One quick Google of "job fair + (university name)" usually yields the numbers/emails required to sign up. Otherwise, calling the Admissions or Career Development offices directly and inquiring about job fairs works too. Also, advertise in collegiate newspapers, on collegiate radio stations, and in "beat" publications (i.e. not just mainstream papers).

There are other ways to get involved and increase your presence with the schools. Some schools offer programs that set up interviews on campus. Students are able to sign up for these interviews online and the rest of the details (room, dates, and timing schedules) are handled by the program. All they need are the businesses. In addition, most schools have organizations on campus that are completely dedicated to professional development. Students love hearing first-hand testimonials about the professions they study. But be warned: these young adults will see through any façade you might present about your job being "great" and "flexible;" trust me when I say that they will be much more receptive toward honesty.

Some professors are very interested in guest lecturers and speakers within the field, because it offers something different to maintain interest and it brings "real-life" experience to the classroom. This can be a little more difficult, but if you have familiarity with the university or college, the Admissions office or academic department chairs can more than likely provide you with a contact to broach this opportunity. You could always emphasize to the professor that you are more than willing to take resumes at the end of class. Not only will this get the students to show up, but they will stay the entire time as well.

2. **Businesses are offering free stuff.** College students *love* anything that's free. So, let's say you have a position that needs to be filled. First, create a meeting (preferably on campus or close to campus) that will outline the employment opportunities within the organization. Second, post flyers around campus for a meeting to discuss this "INCREDIBLE OPPORTUNITY FOR EMPLOYMENT!" You can advertise anywhere: on bulletin boards, above water fountains, at the student recreational rooms, on the back of bathroom stall doors, on chalk boards in classrooms—*be creative!* Third, offer incentives to attend the meeting. Pizza is usually a good bet. One time, I attended a meeting where asking a question (about the company or the product) yielded a $5 reward. Over 300 students were there for close to two hours. That session may have cost the company $150, but it created awareness among 300 students, who more than likely told their friends about how great "such-and-such" company was.

3. **Businesses are reevaluating their environment and avoiding negative experiences**. Keep in mind that there is such a thing as bad publicity. Most college kids really do care what their peers are saying. If someone reports having had a bad experience with an organization or company, and there is no "positive image" rebuttal, the organization is out. Most kids won't even double-check the implications against the business. Furthermore, consider little factors, such as: Are headphones allowed for clerical work? What's

the dress code for the company? (if you don't make it clear, you might be surprised with what is thought of as acceptable)? Is the office rigid and strict or do the employees chat here and there? It's important to weigh whether you're actually going to provide a place where young adults want to work.

If the student is serious about their major, and the job, then s/he will want to learn all aspects of it. So, letting them get involved is important. Student interns are also generally understanding; they realize that they will be doing clerical work, but they also want to attend things like office meetings and client discussions—anything that is really "hands on" to get a good idea about the job. Plus, it would only make them more knowledgeable about the company in the long run.

4. **Businesses are flexible and offering competitive wages.** Sure, most college kids don't hold 9-5 jobs, but they are extremely busy between class, homework, part time jobs, and organizations. Most free time for them is at night (after dinner please, unless you are willing to offer it.) So the businesses that are getting the most attention are offering workshops at 7pm on a Tuesday night. They are interviewing on Saturday afternoons. Sure, it can be a real pain—but the final results are worth it. These kids with jam-packed schedules are not only refining their networking skills, but they are learning the in's and out's of effective time management: a vital skill for the workforce. In addition, college kids aren't too concerned with benefits, so a competitive wage is an incredible incentive.

5. **Businesses are willing to travel.** Large universities and colleges attract students from all over the nation. Be sure to get out of your area and head into new places; those markets are virtually untapped in different regions. For example, Pittsburgh kids might decide to go to Temple (Philadelphia) or Penn State for school, but want to still work at home over summer break. There is a high probability that almost no businesses have even considered advertising and interviewing at alternate locations. This is exceptionally helpful if your company is a chain of stores in both locations. All it takes is one phone call to the area branch office providing contact information and resumes come your way.

At the end of the day, today's upcoming workforce isn't that different from all the other generations. They are willing, able, and excited about applying their knowledge in the field. And the generational differences can easily be thought of as strengths. Today's entering labor force is even *easier* to get into contact with than before. Even though they are always on the go, with the recent explosion of cell phones and wireless technology, this generation is always connected. All today's businesses need to do is sign on.

Weathering the storm

Like it or not, the management style that has worked for the Traditionals and Boomers in the workplace will not succeed as well with the Gen Xers and Gen Yers. The old-fashioned, "Command and Control" hierarchical organizational management style worked well when employees were loyal and employment was a buyer's market. Those days are soon going to be a distant memory. Increasingly, managers are going to have to adapt to the expectations of the younger generations in order to remain competitive in what is swiftly becoming *a seller's job market*.

Furthermore, managers are now going to be faced not just with managing employees from four different generations, but also with managing the *interactions* between the different generations as well. Just when we thought we were getting used to managing gender and ethnic diversity in the workplace, we are faced with addressing age diversity!

Assuming you can only raise wages so much, how else are you going to compete to attract the most talented, skilled, intelligent, and educated workers from the declining work-aged population to your organization?

The answer is, you need to manage skillfully. You need to be resourceful and open to continual learning yourself, just like the younger generations. You need to access the most reliable workforce metrics and seek out pre-employment assessment tools and performance management systems that will enable your business to maintain a competitive advantage. You need to offer attractive incentives to potential new hires, such as "best practice" work environments and opportunities to learn and advance, while retaining your current load of valued contributors.

Productivity is at the heart of any business' ability to compete. Businesses will continue to try and get more output from fewer people. But the ability to increase individual productivity has a limit. How much more can employers squeeze employees without turning off candidates and shedding existing workers?

And that is the crux of the problem facing U.S. employees and employers alike. Employees are being asked to do more, while the number of available workers shrinks. We do not and will not have enough people to fill all the jobs that will be required to provide services and produce goods for a growing, aging, and demanding population—we don't and won't have enough people with the right skills to do all the jobs that exist even today!

But even if we did, these same workers have dependent children and aging relatives who compete for their time. More and more employees are stressed out on the job, resulting in absenteeism, presenteeism, mistakes, accidents, and job-related illnesses. And, as recently as December 2006, one in three workers have been approached by another firm to take them away.

That's bad news for employers, because the "Perfect Labor Storm" has not gone away. It hasn't even fully arrived yet. It just continues to churn and churn, gaining momentum, and heading for a workplace near you. How prepared are you to survive the Perfect Labor Storm if your workplace is at ground zero?

How to make your business "storm-proof"

The coming "Perfect Labor Storm" is inevitable. The colliding demographic forces described in this book have been in place for generations. Your business' response, however, is up to you. In this competitive environment, s/he who hesitates is lost. Employees will soon be in the proverbial "catbird" seat, able to choose from many potential employers. Will they choose your firm?

In 1998, McKinsey and Company described a United States workplace phenomenon known as the "War for Talent," a result of the shortage of workers to fill skilled jobs. McKinsey conducted a yearlong study of 77 companies and 6,600 managers, concluding that the most significant business challenge over the next 20 years will be recruiting, retaining, and inspiring talent. Specifically, companies will find it increasingly difficult to find and keep skilled workers who can perform in a dynamic and global economy, who are technologically savvy, and can adapt quickly to change.

Forty-five years earlier in a speech at Harvard University, Winston Churchill observed that the empires of the future will be empires of the mind. He might have added that the battles of the future will be battles for talent.

"There is nothing new about companies wanting to secure the best talent," opens the article "Everyone's Doing It" in the October 7, 2006 issue of *The Economist*. "The East India Company, founded in 1600, used competitive examinations to recruit alpha minds."

Fortunately, forward-thinking managers and business owners can take the necessary steps to prepare for the tempest. First, you are going to have to "batten down the hatches." You want to go on the defensive by focusing on employee retention. As the storm gathers, employee retention will become more important than ever to the survival of your business. This means guarding against headhunters (as recently as December 2006, one in three workers reported having been approached by another firm to take them away), initiating programs attractive to younger generations, rewarding your high performers, and focusing on providing key employees with rewards and compensation that they value.

In a seller's job market, it will be increasingly critical for employers to understand the motivating factors that drive their employees to want to get up in the morning and come back to work at your organization every day. If you are unable to tap into your employees' core motivating values, you will be unable to retain the best talent within your organization in an increasingly competitive labor marketplace.

My book, *Understanding Business Values and Motivators*, is a highly recommended supplemental resource providing insight and access to the tools you will need to understand your employees' key motivating values, so that you do not risk losing them to your competition.

Once you have "plugged the leaks" in your organization, you can go on the offensive, seeking to identify and attract the best of the available new talent through targeted selection and recruitment efforts. Without a credible plan and the right assessment tools, you risk losing out to your competitors in the predicted war for talent.

Managers who avail themselves of continuing and ongoing knowledge will be best equipped to access numerous resources that will provide them with the knowledge and tools they need to steer their institutional ship successfully through the turbulent waters ahead.

Your Solution: CriteriaOne®: The Whole Person Approach

To remain competitive and profitable, businesses must be able to attract, select, and retain productive workers.

CriteriaOne®: The Whole Person Approach is a cutting-edge process and meta-assessment approach to qualifying candidates for the right jobs and placing them on the right teams and organizations.

CriteriaOne® links individual productivity directly to corporate profitability. It allows managers to seamlessly **benchmark** the profiles of highly successful employees, **evaluate** and **assess** internal and external candidates, and **manage the performance** of all employees.

CriteriaOne® is the solution for businesses committed to thriving during and after the "Perfect Labor Storm."

Revealed through the application of CriteriaOne® are five benefits that help organizations manage costs and maximize individual productivity:

- Hire only people with the potential to succeed.
- Select employees who have the skills to do the job, compatibility to work on a team, and values to fit in the company culture.
- Targeted training, development and coaching resources to improve those skills and behaviors that have the greatest top line/bottom line impact on results.
- Develop an employee evaluation system that encourages ongoing feedback.
- Link individual rewards for productivity and performance improvement to corporate profitability.

About the Author

"Intuitive, practical, and down-to-earth" is the way Dr. Ira Wolfe has been described by clients and colleagues. As founder of Success Performance Solutions, and president of Poised for the Future Company, his approach to employee selection and performance management has earned him the endorsement and respect of both business leaders and peers.

Ira might be best known for the "Perfect Labor Storm" term he coined in 1999, describing events leading up to the largest shortage of skilled workers in American history. Since then he has been speaking, consulting and writing on a regular basis. In addition to writing *The Perfect Labor Storm,* he is also the author of *Understanding Business Values and Motivators.* He is the editor of "The Total View," a weekly e-newsletter with worldwide distribution that discusses hiring, workforce trends and solutions. He also is a columnist for Business2Business Magazine and participates routinely in interviews for the *Wall Street Journal*, BusinessWeekOnline, PCN Cable, regional business publications, and trade publications as well as TV and radio.

While helping a client to build a national sales force in 1999-2000, Ira designed a blueprint for selection, hiring, development, and succession planning, which became CriteriaOne®: The Whole Person Approach, used by dozens of consultants, small businesses, and Fortune 500 companies to reduce turnover, retain employees and improve productivity.

His clients include businesses representing over a dozen industries including healthcare, manufacturing, utilities, retail, distribution, transportation, and call centers. Audiences have included the National Association of Home Builders, Institute of Management Consultants, Material Handling and Logistics Conference, International Dental Congress (Malaysia), VHA, PA Chamber of Commerce, and numerous regional and national business organizations.

Ira is a graduate of Muhlenberg College and the University of Pennsylvania. Currently he is working toward a Masters Degree in Leadership at Duquesne University.

Ira welcomes feedback can be contacted through his corporate websites at *www.super-solutions.com, www.perfectlaborstorm.com,* or via e-mail: *iwolfe@super-solutions.com.*

Contact Dr. Ira S. Wolfe

For information about speaking, management, and employee testing and consulting engagements, Dr. Wolfe can be reached through:
Websites: www.super-solutions.com or www.perfectlaborstorm.com
Email: iwolfe@super-solutions.com or iwolfe@perfectlaborstorm.com
Phone: 1.800.803.4303

FREE weekly updates on the "Perfect Labor Storm" and other stories on how to job-match, manage, and motivate employees. Visit one of the websites listed above and register to receive our weekly e-newsletter, or subscribe to Dr. Wolfe's blog at hrblog.typepad.com/hrblog.

Give the gift of business foresight!

To order additional copies of *The Perfect Labor Storm 2.0*,
Visit *www.perfectlaborstorm.com*

Look for *Understanding Business Values and Motivators*, revised edition, coming soon. To be notified of its release, send an email to: *iwolfe@super-solutions.com*.

Endnotes

1   Kotlikoff, L. and Burns, S. (2005.) *The Coming Generational Storm: What You Need to Know About America's Economic Future*, MIT: Cambridge.

2   Kotlikoff and Burns, pp. 239-240.

3   Kotlikoff and Burns, pp. 239-240.

4   Kotlikoff and Burns, p. 35.

5   Herman, R., Olivo, T., and Gioia, J. (2003.) *Impending Crisis: Too Many Jobs, Too Few People*. Oakhill Press: VA.

6   Kotlikoff and Burns, pp. 4-5.

7   Kotlikoff and Burns, p. 23.

8   Kotlikoff and Burns, 23-24.

9   Deloitte & Touche: *The Future of Health Care: An Outlook from the Perspective of Hospital CEOs*.

10 Marston, p. 180.

11 Marston, p. 180.

12 March 20, 2007. http://www.Trailer-bodybuilders.com

13 Martin, C. and Tulgan, B. (2002.) *Managing the Generation Mix: From Collision to Collaboration*. HRD Press: Amherst, MA.

14 Bennis, W. and Thomas, R. (2002.) *Geeks and Geezers: How Eras, Values, and Defining Moments Shape Leaders*. Harvard Business School Press: Cambridge.

15 Martin and Tulgan, p. 3.

16 Warner, J. and Sandberg, A. (2005.) *Generational Style Assessment (GSA.)* HRD Press: Amherst, MA.

17 Martin, C. and Tulgan, B. (2002.) *Managing the Generation Mix: From Collision to Collaboration*. HRD Press: Amherst, MA, p. 33.

18 Martin and Tulgan, pp. 6-7.

19 Martin and Tulgan, p. 30.

20 Martin and Tulgan, p. 35.

21 Martin and Tulgan, p. 38.

22 Marston, C. (2007.) Motivating the "What's In It For Me" Workforce: Manage Across the Generational Divide and Increase Profits. USA: Wiley, p. 98.

23 Marston, p. 100.

24 Marston, p. 101.

25 Marston, p. 101.

26 Marston, p. 115.

[27] Warner, J. and Sandberg, A. (2005.) *The Generational Style Assessment (GSA.)* HRD Press: Amherst, MA.

[28] Sandberg, A. (2007.) Research on Younger Workers. (Source: PredictSuccess.com)

[29] Marston, p. 99.

[30] Marston, C. (2007.) Motivating the "What's In It For Me" Workforce: Manage Across the Generational Divide and Increase Profits. USA: Wiley, p. 118.

[31] Marston, 120.

[32] Marston, p. 134.

[33] Marston. p 143.

[34] Ad Council. (2007.) *Engaging the Next Generation: How Nonprofits Can Reach Young Adults*, p. 5.

[35] Ad Council, p. 5.

[36] Ad Council, p. 22.

[37] Ad Council, p. 23.

[38] Ad Council, p. 24.

[39] Ad Council, p. 25.

[40] Ad Council, pp. 25, 26.

[41] Ad Council, pp. 26, 27.

[42] Ad Council, p. 28.

[43] Ad Council, p. 31.

[44] Ad Council, p. 31.

[45] Ad Council, p. 29.

References

Ad Council. (2007.) Engaging the Next Generation: How Nonprofits Can Reach Young Adults. Available: www.adcouncil.org.

Bennis, W. and Thomas, R. (2002.) Geeks and Geezers: How Eras, Values, and Defining Moments Shape Leaders. USA: Harvard Business School Press.

Deloitte Consulting LLP and the National Association of Manufacturers' Manufacturing Institute/Center for Workforce Success. 2005 Skills Gap Report-A Survey of the American Manufacturing Workforce

Deloitte Research (2008). It's 2008: Do You Know Where Your Talent Is? Why Acquisition and Retention Strategies Don't Work. New York.

Deloitte Research (2007). Managing the Talent Crisis in Global Manufacturing: Strategies to Attract and Engage Generation Y. New York.

Heet, Justin (2003). Beyond Workforce 2020: The Coming (and Present) International Market for Labor. Hudson Institute, Washington, D.C.

Herman, R. Olivo, T. Gioia, J. (2003.) Impending Crisis: Too Many Jobs, Too Few People. USA: Oakhill Press.

Kotlikoff, L. and Burns, S. (2005.) The Coming Generational Storm: What You Need to Know about America's Economic Future. Cambridge: MIT Press.

Marston, C. (2007.) Motivating the "What's In It for Me" Workforce: Manage Across the Generational Divide and Increase Profits. USA: Wiley.

Martin, C. And Tulgan, B. (2002.) Managing the Generation Mix: From Collision to Collaboration. Amherst, MA: HRD Press.

Press release, America's Aging Workforce Posing New Opportunities and Challenges for Companies (Sept. 19, 2005), Managing the Mature Workforce/Report #1369, The Conference Board.

Watson Wyatt Worldwide (2004). Living Happily Ever After: The Economic Implications of Aging Societies.

Warner, J. and Sandberg, A. (2005.) The Generational Style Assessment (GSA.) Amherst, MA: HRD Press.